JAN RICHARDSON & ELLEN LEWIS

THE NEXT STEP
FORWARD
IN READING
INTERVENTION

The RISE Framework

SCHOLASTIC

CREDITS

Credits: pp. 12, 13, 57: *The Next Step Forward in Guided Reading* copyright © 2016 by Jan Richardson. Published by Scholastic Inc.; p. 70: *Next Step Guided Reading Assessment Grades K–2* copyright © 2013 by Jan Richardson and Maria P. Walther. Published by Scholastic Inc.; pp. 101–102: "The Smuggler" from *Wisdom Tales From Around the World* by Heather Forest. Copyright © 1996 by Heather Forest. Used by permission of August House, Inc.; p. 108: "Building for the Future" from *Guided Reading Short Reads Nonfiction* copyright © 2014 by Scholastic Inc. Published by Scholastic Inc., "Inventing a Game" by Barry Rust from *Storyworks*, November/December 2003. Copyright © 2003 by Scholastic Inc. Published by Scholastic Inc., and "A Walk Through Harlem" from Scholastic *Scope*, February 2010. Copyright © 2010 by Scholastic Inc. Published by Scholastic Inc.; p. 110: *Next Step Guided Reading Assessment Grades 3–5* copyright © 2013 by Jan Richardson and Maria P. Walther. Published by Scholastic Inc.; pp. 117–118: "The Talkative Turtle" from *Wisdom Tales From Around the World* by Heather Forest. Copyright © 1996 by Heather Forest. Used by permission of August House, Inc.; p. 176: *Days With Frog and Toad* copyright © 1979 by Arnold Lobel. Published by Scholastic Inc. by arrangement with HarperCollins Children's Books, a division of HarperCollins Publishers. All rights reserved.

Publisher: Lois Bridges
Editorial director: Sarah Longhi
Development editor: Raymond Coutu
Production editor: Danny Miller
Senior editor: Shelley Griffin
Assistant editor: Molly Bradley
Art director: Brian LaRossa
Interior designer: Maria Lilja

ISBN-13: 978-1-338-29826-0
ISBN-10: 1-338-29826-7

2 3 4 5 6 7 8   123   25 24 23 22 21 20 19

⚠ Text pages printed on 30% PCW recycled paper.

Scholastic Inc., 557 Broadway, New York, NY 10012

To Cecil—my support, my rock, my refuge,
and my loving husband for over 40 years.
—JAN

To Rick, Julie, Katie, Mark, Ruth, and Kathy.
Your love and support mean everything to me.
—ELLEN

Take the **Next Step** Forward
with **Jan Richardson**

The Guided Reading Teacher's Companion and The Next Step Forward in Guided Reading

Improve classroom instruction with these innovative, practical resources and tools based on Jan's Assess-Decide-Guide framework.

The Next Step Forward in Guided Reading: 978-1-338-16111-3
The Guided Reading Teacher's Companion: 978-1-338-16345-2

Next Step Guided Reading in Action

In these video lessons, Jan demonstrates how to plan, teach, check for understanding, and reteach at every reading level. Includes a 64-page View & Do Guide.

Grades K–2: 978-1-338-21734-6
Grades 3 & Up: 978-1-338-21735-3

Next Step Guided Reading Assessment

This streamlined, easy-to-admin assessment captures each reade word knowledge, phonics skills, fluency, and comprehension ski to facilitate data-driven instruct

Grades K–2: 978-0-545-44268-8
Grades 3–6: 978-0-545-44267-1

ACKNOWLEDGMENTS

We owe great thanks to our friend and Title I reading teacher, Angela Kheradmand. Her vision of taking *The Next Step Forward in Guided Reading* plan and segmenting it into a station model for striving readers was the inspiration for the RISE framework.

Thanks to the unwavering support of our Scholastic editorial team, Lois Bridges, Sarah Longhi, and Ray Coutu. They listened to an idea that might change the way intervention happens in schools. Always open to a world of possibilities, they saw the promise of RISE and RISE Up and helped us craft this book to guide fellow educators who want to implement change and break the cycle of ongoing intervention.

Thank you to the amazing team at Springfield Estates Elementary School, Springfield, Virginia, that contributed so much to making RISE and RISE Up a success. Mary, the principal, allowed us to partner with Jan and take risks for children who need that extra burst of intense help. Ellen's RISE team—Debbie, Jill, Susie, and Beth—was indefatigable. Their sense of urgency to make every instructional moment count with kids inspires all who observe their work. Heartfelt kudos to the SEES staff who helped make the filming of instructional video clips happen for both RISE and *The Next Step Forward in Guided Reading*. Thanks to Judy, Cindy, Aaron, Scott, Leslie, Marilyn, and Kathy for their support, suggestions, and friendship.

Thanks to our friends and colleagues in Chattanooga, Tennessee, Deb Rosenow and Jill Levine. Their decades of successful partnering with Jan and their desire to do the very best for all students led them to implement RISE and RISE Up in scores of Hamilton County schools. Hundreds of interventionists, teachers, and literacy specialists embraced RISE and RISE Up with inspiring results—happy, successful readers.

Thanks, too, to our expert tip providers: Debbie Brant, Jessica DeMarco, Leslie Lausten, Jill Northup, Sonal Patel, Deb Rosenow, Beth Samec, and the RISE team at Hartwood Elementary School.

We are grateful to all those who contact us as they implement RISE and RISE Up around the country. We are inspired by your devotion to using Jan's work in the classroom, and now in the intervention setting—and we applaud your successful results for the good of students everywhere.

CONTENTS

Appendices can be downloaded from scholastic.com/NSFIntervention

VIDEOS

Go to scholastic.com/NSFIntervention to access this book's full menu
of professional videos. Watch the authors teach key parts of the interventions.

*Plus, expert reflections,
featuring Jan Richardson,
Ellen Lewis, and other
educators*

"*After spending two years in Tier 3 intervention, Maurion was disengaged, discouraged, and reading eight text levels below the third-grade average. RISE changed Maurion's attitude and achievement. After completing the RISE intervention, he is now a confident, on-grade-level reader who begs his teacher to let him read more in class!*"

—**JESSICA DEMARCO**, guided reading specialist and RISE instructor,
Calvin Donaldson Elementary School, Chattanooga, Tennessee

"*The RISE and RISE Up interventions have been incredibly successful. Student motivation and engagement have been phenomenal. In eight weeks, 10 of our 12 RISE students met the benchmark for their grade. The round-2 RISE group, composed of all ELL students, soared. My principal couldn't be happier, and as a reading specialist, I am also seeing the benefits of RISE to classroom teachers, who have never before felt this level of support. With RISE and RISE Up, we are able to serve more students. We are excited to increase not only our efficiency, but also our effectiveness in meeting students' reading needs.*"

—**MARILYN MINER**, reading teacher, Reading Recovery teacher,
and ELL teacher, North Springfield Elementary School, Virginia

"*Students stop me in the hallway on a regular basis and ask, 'When can I come to RISE?' or 'How can I get into RISE? Do you have space for me?' Students who have 'graduated' from RISE ask, 'When can I come back?' RISE has truly changed the face of intervention at our school.*"

—**RANITA GLENN**, reading specialist and RISE instructor,
Hardy Elementary School, Chattanooga, Tennessee

"*I have never seen student growth like we have this year! In fact, most of our participating students have grown multiple reading levels within just a couple of months utilizing this innovative approach. As a principal who is leading a Title I school, I could not imagine using any other instructional model for our students and wonder why we did not implement this sooner!*"

—**SCOTT ELCHENKO**, principal, Harwood Elementary
School, Stafford County, Virginia

Introduction

Teachers are passionate about helping children who struggle with reading, yet too often we see those children spend months or even years in intervention programs that rarely help them reach proficiency. They're shuffled from one program to the next and never make the sustained gains necessary to free them from the chains of intervention. All that is about to change.

THE RISE FRAMEWORK: A MAJOR STEP FORWARD IN READING INTERVENTION

This book is about RISE (Reading Intervention for Students to Excel), a powerful, short-term intervention for children in grades 1 to 8. Because RISE is intense and fast-paced, we do not recommend it for kindergarten students. They should receive a comprehensive literacy program that includes reading, writing, phonics, listening, and speaking. Children who cannot identify at least 40 upper- and lowercase letters (pre-A level) should also receive individual and small-group instruction to support their developing literacy skills. They should be immersed in a print-rich literacy program with lots of opportunities to engage with books—interactive read-aloud, shared reading, and time to explore books on their own in the classroom library.

We also use two activities to quickly accelerate pre-A students: tracing an ABC book with a tutor, and pre-A small-group lessons (Richardson, 2016). Even in Title I schools with a high percentage of children living in poverty and/or emerging bilinguals, our research shows that students who receive these two instructional interventions quickly catch up to their peers and complete kindergarten on track.

Three things make RISE powerful: the lesson framework of *The Next Step Forward in Guided Reading*, the children's engagement and guided practice with the task, and the RISE teacher team collaboration. And, of course, RISE works best—and all children thrive—with daily, high-quality classroom literacy instruction.

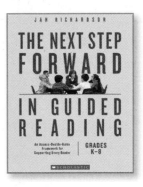

Field tests have shown remarkable results—data from over 1,000 students in more than 20 schools indicate that the average lift from RISE is one text level every two weeks! Go to scholastic.com/NSFIntervention to see the exciting findings of an ongoing action research study.

WHY DID WE WRITE THIS BOOK?

We wrote this book for separate but complementary reasons.

Jan's Reasons

I have worked in the field of literacy for more than three decades—as a classroom teacher, Title I teacher, reading specialist, Reading Recovery® teacher leader, researcher, professor, author, and literacy consultant. I've taught hundreds and hundreds of small-group guided reading lessons and have seen thousands of children accelerate. Few things in life bring me more joy than seeing a striving reader thrive. I love it. I absolutely love it.

Why do so many interventions fail to accelerate striving readers? There are several reasons. In many cases, the intervention lesson is fragmented. It focuses on only one aspect of the reading process, such as phonemic awareness, fluency, or decoding, but the student isn't given the assistance he or she needs to transfer the isolated skills to authentic reading and writing.

Another reason children don't accelerate is the school day does not contain enough "eyes on text" reading. The guided reading lesson may not have enough reading and writing. Additionally, too often, striving readers are assigned independent activities that are too difficult, or they are easily distracted and can't stay on task without constant monitoring.

Another issue is teacher collaboration—or lack thereof! Many teachers with whom I've worked have expressed concern that the instruction striving readers receive is not coordinated. The intervention teacher may be doing something completely different, for instance, from what the classroom teacher is doing. I'm not blaming the teachers. Teachers work hard, and sometimes there just isn't enough time in the school day for them to collaborate on individual students. But teacher collaboration is critical for an effective intervention program.

In the intermediate grades, the biggest acceleration challenge for striving readers is comprehension. Most can decode well and read with fluency and phrasing, but they have difficulty understanding texts deeply. Interventions need to include explicit teaching, differentiated coaching, and supportive practice around comprehension needs—and the fact is, most don't.

"Is it possible to provide a short-term intervention that rescues striving readers from the cycle of frustration and failure?

Yes! RISE and RISE Up can end the cycle!"

The underlying question remains the same: Is it possible to provide a short-term intervention that rescues striving readers from the cycle of frustration and failure?

Yes! RISE and RISE Up can end the cycle! The interventions detailed in this book offer intensive, short-term, targeted instruction in reading, writing, word study, and comprehension. After a couple months of intervention, students gain the confidence, proficiency, and skills they need to excel as readers and exit intervention once and for all!

Ellen's Reasons

As a Reading Recovery® teacher, literacy leader, and consultant, I have worked with striving readers for more than three decades in schools from Bermuda to England, to the Far East, the Middle East, and throughout the United States. The common thread among those students is the desire to overcome their literacy challenges. They desperately want to be better readers. They want to be part of their class and not singled out for special programs. They don't want to embarrass themselves or find themselves lost when their classmates are happily reading and discussing texts. They want to read all the different kinds of texts they see their friends reading and enjoying.

Many striving readers feel like lifetime members of the reading intervention club. They have spent years in a variety of pullout groups. Although those students may accelerate, I've noticed that they often don't sustain their gains once back in the classroom. Again and again, I have asked myself what I can do to help them. The answer has come from Jan's work.

For years, I've partnered with Jan to implement her theory and practice in Title I schools. I've seen firsthand what a positive impact her work has had on classroom practice, particularly small-group reading instruction.

Then, several years ago, Angela Kheradmand, a fellow reading teacher and friend, thought of compressing Jan's two-day lesson framework from *The Next Step Forward in Guided Reading* into a 45- to 60-minute intensive intervention, moving readers through four stations that target each of Jan's lesson components. That became the basis for RISE.

four stations that target each of Jan's lesson components. That became the basis for RISE. Then, a few years later, we developed an intervention for intermediate students called RISE Up, which is based on the strategies and modules in Chapter 7 of *The Next Step Forward in Guided Reading*.

The literacy team at my school, Springfield Estates Elementary in Springfield, Virginia, implemented RISE in first and second grade—and the results were stunning! Striving readers began to actively problem-solve unknown words, and we saw their reading levels elevated every two weeks. Most significantly, after only eight weeks of intervention, the students maintained their gains and thrived in their classrooms.

This handbook is our step-by-step guide for literacy leaders, teachers, and administrators who are looking for a reading intervention program that works.

CHAPTER 1

The Roots of RISE and RISE Up

The idea for RISE was developed by Angela Kheradmand, a Title I reading teacher in Fairfax County, Virginia. She attended a training session led by Jan and brought with her a team of first-grade, Title I reading and ELL teachers.

After attending the session, Angela and her team implemented Jan's guided reading lesson framework and saw powerful, positive results. However, they were serving many students who struggled to read and, therefore, they needed a way to transform guided reading instruction into an intervention program. Angela thought of compressing Jan's two-day lesson framework from *The Next Step Forward in Guided Reading* (Richardson, 2016) into a one-day 45- to 60-minute intervention that included 15 minutes of instruction in all four components: Read a New Book, Phonics and Word Study, Reread Yesterday's Book, and Guided Writing. A different instructor would be responsible for teaching each of the four stations as small groups of striving readers rotated through them. She thought this model might result in accelerated progress. She was right! The intensive, targeted intervention worked better than anyone could have imagined. Angela shared the results with Ellen and her team at Springfield Estates Elementary School.

ELLEN IMPLEMENTS RISE

My school was already a "Jan plan school," implementing the ideas in *The Next Step Forward in Guided Reading* in all K–6 classrooms, but my colleagues and I wanted more for the students who wound up in one or another intervention program, year after year.

We adapted the intervention for our school. We started by using RISE in first and second grades, using all the resources we had: specialists, teaching assistants, supportive administrators, and good leveled books for guided reading. During that time, Jan was partnering with our school, providing professional development workshops on guided reading. I showed her the data we had on the RISE students' performance. She reviewed the work, observed the lessons, and partnered with us to design the most effective strategies for each station.

The partnership of classroom teachers and interventionists using Jan's work with fidelity was key to our success. We watched striving readers move up in reading levels every two weeks as they began to problem-solve unknown words. Most significantly, after only eight weeks, the students exited RISE and thrived in their classrooms. Most did not need any further intervention for the rest of the year—or the next! My colleagues and I were further amazed when, at the beginning of the following school year, we realized that every single RISE student maintained his or her gains without attending summer school.

Word spread about the program. Imagine their excitement when reading teachers and literacy leaders heard that there is a reading intervention program that *actually* works!

Educators began requesting visits to our school to watch RISE in action. The majority decided to implement a RISE program in their own schools.

AND THEN CAME RISE UP

The next step was to find a solution for our upper-grade students who struggled with comprehension. In a professional development session at our school, Jan taught guided reading lessons to students who were good decoders but had difficulty understanding texts at deeper levels. Using the same short text, she modeled how to teach two different strategies. In the first lesson, she taught students how to identify important details in a story, and in the second, she taught them how to analyze characters to determine feelings and traits. By applying more than one comprehension strategy to the same text, students were forced to think flexibly and more deeply. They were also more analytical when discussing the text. Their written responses became more complex and reflected their deeper thinking.

In the months that followed, Jan worked with our literacy team to develop a 45-minute intervention exclusively for intermediate students who needed to improve their comprehension skills. We conferred with teachers and chose 12 students who could decode on or near grade level but struggled with comprehension. We divided the students into three groups and rotated them through three stations, each led by a different instructor. At each station, they practiced a different comprehension strategy on a short text. We named this intervention RISE Up.

After eight weeks of RISE Up lessons, the students returned to their classroom guided reading groups with stronger comprehension skills. And the majority of these

Springfield Estates Elementary School in Virginia is a National Blue Ribbon School, largely because of the strides children made with RISE.

 The Next Step Forward in Reading Intervention © 2018 by Jan Richardson and Ellen Lewis. Published by Scholastic Inc.

After eight weeks of RISE Up lessons, the students returned to their classroom guided reading groups with stronger comprehension skills. And the majority of these students, who had never passed a state reading test, were successful for the first time. All of them passed *both* the decoding and comprehension sections of the *Developmental Reading Assessment* (Beaver, 2012) and the *Next Step Guided Reading Assessment* (Richardson & Walther, 2013). The teachers were convinced that RISE Up made the difference.

After implementing RISE and RISE Up for three years, we became a National Blue Ribbon School. The principal, Mary Randolph, who supported and encouraged our literacy team, cited the implementation of RISE as a major reason we were able to "close the gap" with our minority students.

Struggling vs. Striving

Stephanie Harvey and Annie Ward write in From Striving to Thriving: How to Grow Confident, Capable Readers, *"We replace the dooming label 'struggling readers' with the effort-based term 'striving readers' because it connotes energy, action, and progress. We feel urgency and agency about matching striving readers with compelling reading materials, arranging time and space to read a lot, and providing expert instruction" (Harvey & Ward, 2017). We agree and believe deeply that the RISE framework is the best and most efficient way to help all striving readers become thriving readers.*

RISE AND RISE UP ARE SPREADING

Today, RISE and RISE Up are being used with thousands of students in schools throughout America. And now, we want to share these wonderful interventions with you. This handbook is a step-by-step guide for literacy leaders, teachers, and administrators looking for a new response to intervention. We urge you to read the following chapters and give RISE and/or RISE Up a try. You will see a positive impact in children's literacy lives!

HOW THIS BOOK IS ORGANIZED

- Chapters 2 and 3 focus on the RISE framework, explaining in detail what it is and how to implement it.

- Chapters 4 and 5 explain the RISE Up framework.

- Chapter 6 describes RISE With Literacy, an after-school event you can use to introduce parents to the strategies taught in the RISE lessons.

- The Appendices are loaded with practical resources such as lesson templates, Comprehension Cards, and tools for communicating with parents.

CHAPTER 2

What Is RISE?

RISE is a tested and proven intensive literacy intervention based on Jan's guided reading lesson framework and implemented 45 to 60 minutes a day for six to eight weeks. It is designed for children in grades 1 to 5 reading at text levels C–N who need to improve decoding, spelling, fluency, writing, and retelling. Our research based on field-testing showed students who participated in six to eight weeks of RISE made 6.4 months of progress and showed significant improvement in comprehension, as measured on *Next Step Guided Reading Assessment* (Richardson & Walther, 2013) and *Benchmark Assessment System* (Fountas & Pinnell, 2016). For students who read above level N and only need to improve their comprehension, use the RISE Up procedures described in Chapters 4 and 5.

There is no reading without comprehension; we want students to understand that reading is a process of constructing meaning from text. While they are reading, they should always ask themselves, "Does this make sense?" If it doesn't, we want them to have a variety of strategies to construct meaning. RISE and RISE Up marshal the full force of language—reading, writing, speaking, and listening. In every intervention session, students are supported by all four language processes.

HOW DOES RISE WORK?

The literacy team and the classroom teachers use assessments to select up to 16 students who need intervention and who read at about the same text level. Those students are placed in smaller groups of three or four and rotate through four instructional stations. Each station is led by an instructor and targets one of Jan's lesson components: reading a new book, word study, rereading and discussing the book, and guided writing.

The RISE leader should be a credentialed teacher—ideally a reading specialist or Reading Recovery® teacher who can train the other members of the team, monitor student progress, assist with lesson planning, and communicate with classroom teachers. The other RISE instructors can be special-education teachers, Title I teachers, reading interventionists, ELL teachers, literacy coaches, retired teachers, student teachers, teaching assistants, or other adults who routinely work with students in your school.

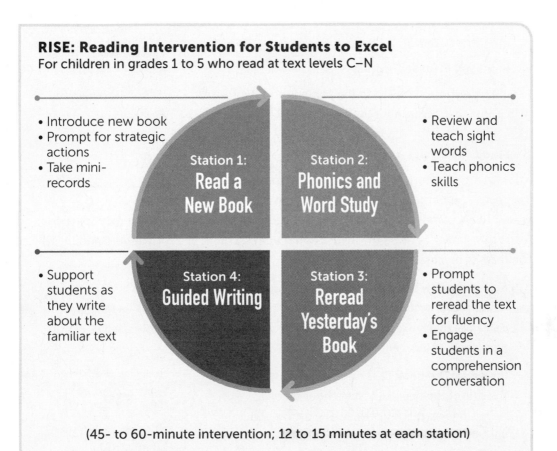

RISE: Reading Intervention for Students to Excel
For children in grades 1 to 5 who read at text levels C–N

- Introduce new book
- Prompt for strategic actions
- Take mini-records

Station 1:
Read a New Book

Station 2:
Phonics and Word Study

- Review and teach sight words
- Teach phonics skills

- Support students as they write about the familiar text

Station 4:
Guided Writing

Station 3:
Reread Yesterday's Book

- Prompt students to reread the text for fluency
- Engage students in a comprehension conversation

(45- to 60-minute intervention; 12 to 15 minutes at each station)

THE RISE STATIONS

Groups of three or four students rotate through four instructional stations:

- Station 1: Read a New Book
- Station 2: Phonics and Word Study
- Station 3: Reread Yesterday's Book
- Station 4: Guided Writing

In this section, we describe the stations and the instruction that occurs at each.

TIP

Assign each station a color, perhaps those in the chart on page 21. Then attach an appropriately colored balloon to each station. This helps children know which station to go to next.

Station 1: Read a New Book

At Station 1, students read a new book with prompting. The focus is monitoring, problem-solving unknown words, fluency, and comprehension. It is best if a reading teacher or literacy specialist leads this station because the instruction requires a more in-depth understanding of the reading process.

1. **Select the new book.** Choose a short, engaging book at the group's instructional reading level as determined by a leveled reading assessment such as *Next Step Guided Reading Assessment, Developmental Reading Assessment* (Beaver, 2012), or *Benchmark Assessment System* (Fountas & Pinnell, 2016).

2. **Introduce the book (2–3 minutes).** Tell students the title of the book and give a brief synopsis. Have students quickly preview the pictures while you call attention to new and important words that might be challenging for them to decode. Limit teacher talk. The introduction should take no more than three minutes.

3. **Students read with prompting (8–10 minutes).** Students read independently while you work with each one individually. Do not choral read or use round-robin reading. Students should reread the book if they finish before time is up.

4. **Take mini-records.** As each student reads a page or two, listen and take notes (mini-records) in the boxes provided on the lesson plan. (See pages 24 to 25 and Appendix A for the lesson plan.) Mini-records resemble

TIP

Keep the book introduction brief. After giving a simple statement describing the gist of the story, let the children preview the book. Discuss new vocabulary when you encounter it during the preview.

running records, but unlike running records, you can interrupt the student to prompt or to demonstrate a strategy. The teacher records a check mark if the student reads the word accurately. She or he also notes the child's fluency and records miscues, rereading, insertions, omissions, and self-corrections. (See sample mini-records on page 25.) The mini-record results can be used to identify teaching points and prompts based on students' needs. They can also be used to plan the next few lessons. When students are reading with phrasing and fluency without making many errors, it is time to give them a higher-level book.

 TIP

Be sure to take a mini-record on every child and use those records to inform your team meeting discussion— and to drive what you teach each child.

5. **Teach a strategy (1–2 minutes).** Spend the final minute or two demonstrating a word-solving strategy to the group. Select a challenging word from the book and write it on the dry-erase board. Demonstrate how to decode it by sounding the first part, covering the ending, finding a known part, or using the rime.

See pages 125 and 178 for examples of other teaching points for early and transitional readers.

VIDEO LINK

Station 1: Read a New Book

You will not have much time to discuss the book at this station. However, students will reread the book and discuss it the following day at the Reread Yesterday's Book Station. When the chime or bell rings, students move to the next station. If they are taking the book home, remind them to bring it back the next day.

RISE Station 1 Lesson Plan: Read a New Book

Students read a new book with teacher prompting.

Book Title	Level	Date
The Three Billy Goats	E	11/2

Brief Synopsis

The three billy goat brothers want to cross the bridge to eat grass on the other side, but the mean troll does not want them to!

New Vocabulary and Language

troll, p. 3   first, p. 5   more, p. 14   big→bigger → biggest, p. 4

Monitoring and Word-Solving Prompts

☐ Are you right?

☐ Does that make sense (or look right)?

☑ Reread and sound the first part.

☑ What would make sense and look right?

☑ Check the middle (or end) of the word.

☐ Find the magic rime.

☐ Cover the ending. Find a part you know.

☐ Do you know another word that looks like this one?

☐ Try the other vowel sound.

☑ Use a known part. big (bigger)

☐ Look all the way to the end of the word.

See *The Next Step Forward in Guided Reading*, pages 125 and 178, for additional prompts.

Fluency Prompts

☑ Don't point. Read it faster.

☐ Read it the way the character would say it.

☐ Read that again while I use my fingers to frame a few words at a time.

☐ How would you say that bold word?

☐ Did you notice that period (or question mark)? Read that again.

☐ Read it while I use my finger to help you read a bit faster. (Use finger to mask the text.)

Comprehension Prompts

☐ What did you read?

☑ What are you thinking?

☐ What's the problem in the story?

☑ How is the character feeling now? Why?

☐ What have you learned?

Appendix A and scholastic.com/NSFIntervention

RISE Station 1 Lesson Plan: Read a New Book

Take mini-records. Record observations and next steps for individual students.

Name: Mia ✓✓✓✓✓ went|SC
✓✓✓✓✓✓ take |SC
✓✓✓✓ trick   Praise: SC

Name: Mariana ✓✓ — three ✓✓
✓✓✓✓✓✓

Name: Yaza ✓✓✓ goat / goats
✓✓✓✓
✓✓ Prompt: ✓ the end

Name: Adriel ✓✓✓✓✓
were / are ✓✓✓✓ on / over ✓
Prompt: Reread — are you right?

Name: Sam ✓✓✓✓
✓✓✓✓✓✓✓ the / a   won't / will not
✓✓✓

Name: Danya ✓✓✓✓ R ✓✓✓
✓✓✓ R ✓✓✓✓✓✓✓
Slow but accurate
reread to confirm w/o prompting

Name: Julian ✓ went / want ✓✓✓ — the
✓✓✓✓ the / a ✓✓✓✓✓ go
Prompt: slow down and monitor.

Name: Mai ✓✓✓✓
✓ were / are ✓✓ went / want
Prompt: Does it make sense?

Name: Soleana ✓✓✓
✓✓✓ on / to ✓✓✓✓✓✓✓

Name: Miriam (inserts words)
✓✓ big ✓✓✓✓✓✓
✓✓✓ ✓✓✓ — too Prompt: Does it look right?

Name: Daniel ✓✓✓✓✓
✓✓ br-others / brothers ✓ ✓✓
Praise: Took word apart

Name: Haset ✓✓✓✓✓
✓✓ a / the ✓✓✓✓✓
Prompt: read it like the character

Name:

Name:

Name:

Name:

Notes From Daily Debriefing

Ready to move to next text level.
Continue to prompt for expression.

Appendix A and scholastic.com/NSFIntervention

Station 2: Phonics and Word Study

At this station, students learn developmentally appropriate sight words and phonics skills. Assess students using the Sight Word Charts for Monitoring Progress (Appendix G) and the Word Knowledge Inventory (Appendix H). Then use the results to identify words and skills to teach. Spend the first five minutes on sight words and the last 10 doing word study activities that target needed skills. Below is a brief description of each activity.

Appendix H and scholastic.com/NSFIntervention

Sight Words

Students learn a new sight word and review words that have been recently taught.

1. **Review sight words (1–2 minutes).** Distribute small dry-erase boards and markers to students. Dictate three familiar words from a Sight Word Chart (Appendix G) for students to write. This is not a test. Help students if they need it. If a student is able to write a word without help, check off that word on the Sight Word Chart.

Appendix G and scholastic.com/NSFIntervention

The Next Step Forward in Reading Intervention © 2018 by Jan Richardson and Ellen Lewis. Published by Scholastic Inc.

2. **Teach a new sight word (3 minutes).** From the text, select a new sight word that students don't know how to write. (Refer to the Sight Word Charts to identify words to teach at each level.) The following four-step procedure helps students develop visual memory, establish left-to-right visual scanning skills, and increase automatic recall of sight words. Do the steps in order and do not skip any of them. Remember, you are not just teaching a word, you are teaching students a system for remembering words.

> ☀ **TIP**
>
> *Teach students to check the word by running a finger under it as they say it in a natural way. This reinforces left-to-right visual scanning and promotes the integration of visual and auditory processing skills.*

- **What's Missing?** Write the word on a dry-erase board (or make the word with magnetic letters) and ask students to look at each letter as you slide an index card, left to right, across the word. Turn the board toward you and erase (or remove) a letter. Show the board to the students and ask, "What's missing?" When students say the missing letter, put it back into the word. Repeat the procedure two or three times, erasing more letters each time until you've erased the entire word. Then have students call out each of the word's letters in order as you write them on the board.

- **Mix and Fix.** Give students magnetic letters to make the new word. Keep the word on the dry-erase board in case students need a reference. After students make the word, have them slide their finger under the word and check it for accuracy. Have students say the word as they check it, but discourage them from segmenting each sound. Next, have them push the letters up one at a time. Then have students mix up the letters and remake the word, from left to right. Keep the word on the table and cover it with an index card.

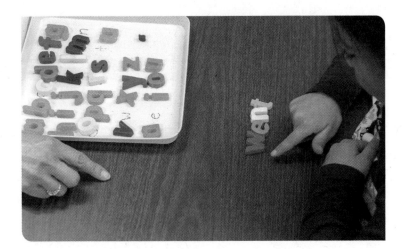

RISE

- **Table Writing.** Ask students to "write" the word on the table with their index finger. Make sure they are looking at their finger while they write. This helps build a memory trace for the word.

- **Write and Retrieve.** Have students write the new word on a dry-erase board as they say it softly. Do not allow students to spell or sound out the word. You want them to learn it as a complete unit. If students leave out an easy-to-hear letter, have them say the word softly as they check it with their finger. After they write the word, have them erase it. Now dictate a very familiar word they know how to write. Check and erase. Finally, dictate the new sight word for them to retrieve from memory and write.

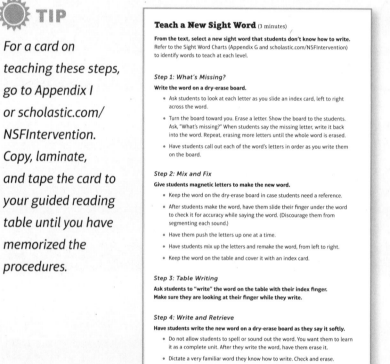

 TIP

For a card on teaching these steps, go to Appendix I or scholastic.com/ NSFIntervention. Copy, laminate, and tape the card to your guided reading table until you have memorized the procedures.

Teach a New Sight Word (3 minutes)

From the text, select a new sight word that students don't know how to write. Refer to the Sight Word Charts (Appendix G and scholastic.com/NSFIntervention) to identify words to teach at each level.

Step 1: What's Missing?
Write the word on a dry-erase board.
- Ask students to look at each letter as you slide an index card, left to right across the word.
- Turn the board toward you. Erase a letter. Show the board to the students. Ask, "What's missing?" When students say the missing letter, write it back into the word. Repeat, erasing more letters until the whole word is erased.
- Have students call out each of the word's letters in order as you write them on the board.

Step 2: Mix and Fix
Give students magnetic letters to make the new word.
- Keep the word on the dry-erase board in case students need a reference.
- After students make the word, have them slide their finger under the word to check it for accuracy while saying the word. (Discourage them from segmenting each sound.)
- Have them push the letters up one at a time.
- Have students mix up the letters and remake the word, from left to right.
- Keep the word on the table and cover it with an index card.

Step 3: Table Writing
Ask students to "write" the word on the table with their index finger. Make sure they are looking at their finger while they write.

Step 4: Write and Retrieve
Have students write the new word on a dry-erase board as they say it softly.
- Do not allow students to spell or sound out the word. You want them to learn it as a complete unit. After they write the word, have them erase it.
- Dictate a very familiar word they know how to write. Check and erase.
- Dictate the new sight word for them to retrieve from memory and write.

▶ VIDEO LINK

Station 2: Phonics and Word Study

Rime Magic for RISE *(3–5 minutes)*

This next activity is based on onset/rime research (Goswami & Bryant, 1990) and Sharon Zinke's Rime Magic program (2017). A syllable can normally be divided into two parts: the onset, which consists of the initial consonant or consonant cluster, and the rime, which consists of the vowel and any final consonants. For instance, in the word *chin*, *ch* is the onset and *in* is the rime. We have adapted activities from Rime Magic that are appropriate for students reading texts at levels C–N.

Make cards for the short vowels, rimes, words, and endings in Appendix J. Spend three to five minutes each day on one of the following steps. Begin with Step 1 and don't move to the next step until students demonstrate mastery of the current one.

Review short vowel sounds and read Magic Rimes. Show students the Short Vowel Strip. As you point to each letter, students say the short vowel twice and the picture: "…/a/, /a/, apple, " "…/e/, /e/, egg, " "…/i/, /i/, igloo, " "…/o/, /o/, octopus, " "…/u/, /u/, umbrella." At first you may need to say the sounds with the students, but gradually you can release your support so students do the work.

A	E	I	O	U

ab	at	id	ob	ub
ad	ed	ig	od	ud
ag	em	im	og	ug
am	en	in	op	um
an	et	ip	ot	un
ap	ib	it	om	ut

After practicing the short vowel sounds, have students read the Magic Rimes. Hold up each two-letter rime card and have students say the rime twice (e.g., *ug-ug*). If students hesitate, cover the consonant and direct them to use the Short Vowel Strip to make the initial vowel sound. Then reveal the consonant and have them say the rime. Continue the procedures with other rime cards.

Appendix J and scholastic.com/ NSFIntervention

3. **Spell and write one-syllable words with Magic Rimes.** Shuffle the rime cards. Show students a card and have them read it. Then, ask them to spell a word with a single initial consonant (e.g., *ug...ug...spell "bug"*). Place one finger in front of *ug* to represent the onset (*b*). After students spell the word, show them a different two-letter rime card and repeat the process. Once students are proficient at spelling words with a single-letter onset, have them spell words with two-letter onsets (e.g., *sl-ug*). Occasionally, have students spell words with three-letter onsets (e.g., *spr-ig*, *spl-it*). There are suggested words in Appendix J. Every once in a while, have students write one of the dictated words on their dry-erase boards. This helps you see which students understand the process and which ones need more support.

4. **Read one-syllable words with Magic Rimes.** Write some of the one-syllable words from Appendix J on 3-x-5 cards. Hold up a word card and ask students to read it. If they struggle, tell them to break the word at the rime (e.g., *cl-ap*). Then have them read the word. Continue with other one-syllable word cards.

5. **Spell and write words with endings.** Show students the Endings Card and read it together (___ed, ___ing, ___er, ___est, ___y, ___le). Hold up a rime card and show students how to spell a word with an onset and one of the endings. Tell them they will always double the consonant when they add an ending to the rime (e.g., *ip...ip...spell slipper...s-l-i-p-p-e-r*). Use your fingers to represent the number of letters they need to add to the rime. Show students other rime cards and dictate a word with an ending for students to spell or write on dry-erase boards. (Suggested words for each rime are listed on pages 151 to 152.)

6. **Read words with endings.** Write some of the words with endings from Appendix J on 8-x-2 cards. Hold up a word card and ask students to read it. If needed, prompt them to break the word apart at the rime and the ending. You can also use your hands to surround the rime (e.g., *ip* in *slipping*). Then take away your right hand so students can read the onset and rime (*slip*). Finally, remove your left hand so students see the word with the ending (*slipping*). Once your students master these skills, you can find more challenging activities in *Rime Magic* (Zinke, 2017).

Other Word Study Activities *(5–7 minutes)*

During the remaining time at this station, do one or two word study activities from the lesson plan: Picture Sorting, Making Words, Sound Boxes, Analogy Charts, Breaking Words, Make a Big Word, or Make Spelling/Meaning Connections. (See Appendix B and scholastic.com/NSFIntervention for the lesson plan.) Each activity addresses an aspect of phonemic awareness and phonics.

Word Study Activities and Their Purposes	
Activity	**Purpose**
Picture Sorting	Learn target sounds.
Making Words	Use sounds to monitor for visual information during reading. Use onset/rime to break words apart.
Sound Boxes	Hear sounds in words and record them in sequence.
Analogy Charts	Use familiar words (e.g., *day*) to solve unfamiliar words (e.g., *stay*, *today*). Analogy Charts are especially good for teaching the silent *e* feature and complex vowel patterns such as *oi*, *ou*, and *ew*.
Breaking Words	Learn how to take words apart while reading.
Make a Big Word	Spell and read multisyllabic words.
Make Spelling/ Meaning Connections	Use known parts of words to read and write new words.

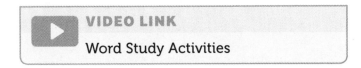

VIDEO LINK
Word Study Activities

Select a target skill. Use students' reading and spelling errors or the Word Knowledge Inventory to identify a target skill. You will likely focus on the same target skill for the entire week. The following chart recommends target skills for each text level.

Target Skills for Each Text Level	
Text Level	**Target Skill**
C	Short, medial vowels. Hearing and recording CVC words
D	Digraphs
E	Initial blends
F	Final blends
G–H	Silent *e* feature and easy vowel combinations: *ay, all, ar, or, ee, oo, er, ow*
I–J	More complex vowel combinations: *oa, ai, ea, ou, ew, oy, aw, igh*
K–L	Adding inflectional endings and multisyllabic words
M–N	Making spelling/meaning connections

 The Next Step Forward in Reading Intervention © 2018 by Jan Richardson and Ellen Lewis. Published by Scholastic Inc.

Picture Sorting

For Picture Sorting, always select two examples of the target skill. If your target skill is hearing medial short vowels, for instance, you might have students sort pictures that have a short *a* and a short *i*. When working with digraphs, you might choose *th* and *ch* as your examples.

To teach students how to hear consonant blends, choose two blends that begin with the same letter (e.g., *cl-cr* or *st-sl*). Students then sort pictures that begin with these blends. Selecting blends that begin with the same letter helps students attend to the second letter in the blend, which is the most challenging for them to hear.

After you distribute three or four pictures to each student, write the target skills on a dry-erase board or easel. Have students take turns sorting their pictures as they follow these procedures:

1. Say the word in the picture: *snake*.

2. Say the first part: *sn*.

3. Say the letters that make that sound: *s-n*.

4. Put the picture under the blend *sn*.

Making Words

Each student will need magnetic letters to make a series of words. If you have a tray of magnetic letters for each student, you won't need to take time gathering letters. Magnetic letters and printed trays are available at teacher stores and online. Metal stove burner covers will also work. Just be sure to write the alphabet on the stove burner cover with a permanent marker so students can replace the letters after they use them.

Dictate a series of words that differ by one or two letters. After students make each word, have them break apart the onset and rime (e.g., *cl-ap*) and point to each part as they say it.

Making Words Activities by Skill Focus

Skill Focus	Making Words Activities	Letters Needed
Short vowels	can-cap-map-mop-top-tap	a, c, m, n, o, p, t
	lip-lap-lid-lad-mad-mud	a, d, i, l, m, p, u
	run-bun-bin-bit-bet-but	b, e, i, n, r, t, u
	got-get-net-pet-pat	a, e, g, n, o, p, t
Digraphs	hip-chip-chop-shop-ship	c, h, i, o, p, s
	bat-bath-math-mash-mush	a, b, h, m, s, t
	cat-chat-that-than-thin	a, c, h, n, t
	dish-dash-bash-mash-mush-much-such	a, b, c, d, h, i, m, s, u
Initial blends	plum-drum-drug-snug-snag	a, d, g, l, m, n, p, r, s, u
	win-twin-twig-swig-swim	g, i, m, n, s, t, w
	stab-stub-grub-gram-glam-glum	a, b, g, l, m, r, s, t, u
	rim-trim-trip-trap-strap-strip	a, i, m, p, r, s, t
Final blends	fat-fast-last-lest-left-lent	a, e, f, l, n, s, t
	rat-rant-pant-past-pest	a, e, n, p, r, s, t
	bang-bank-band-land	a, b, d, g, k, l, n
	milk-silk-silt-wilt	i, k, l, m, s, t, w
Initial and final blends	ran-ranch-branch-brunch	a, b, c, h, n, r, u
	rink-shrink-think-chink-chunk	c, h, i, k, n, r, s, u
	pit-spit-split-splint-sprint	i, l, n, p, r, s, t
	rest-quest-chest-check-chick-quick	c, c, e, h, i, k, q, r, s, t, u

 The Next Step Forward in Reading Intervention © 2018 by Jan Richardson and Ellen Lewis. Published by Scholastic Inc.

Sound Boxes

Each student needs a Sound Box Template (Appendix K) inserted into a plastic sheet protector, a dry-erase marker, and an eraser. Dictate a phonetic word that contains a target skill the students need to learn (short vowel, digraph, or blend). Tell students how many boxes they will need. Because the goal of this activity is phonetic spelling, avoid words with silent letters. Have students say the word slowly and run their finger under the boxes. Then have them say the word again as they write the letters in the boxes. After they write each word, have them check the letters and sounds by saying the word slowly as they run their finger under the word. When you use words with digraphs, the two letters for the digraph will go in the same box because they represent one sound or phoneme (e.g., *ch, th, sh, ck*). Because blends have two phonemes, each letter of a blend goes into a separate box (e.g., *br, sp, fl, cr*).

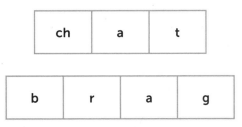

Examples of Words for Sound Boxes	
Focus	**Examples**
Short vowels	map, tag, sit, net, mob, get, cap, rid, hop, run, gum
Digraphs	math, chin, such, chat, chop, such, back, hush, ship
Initial blends	brag, flap, sped, clam, grin, sled, crab, clip, drop, spun
Final blends	rung, dusk, task, land, pink, film, milk, lump, kept, gust
Initial and final blends	clash, skunk, crush, shaft, plump, chomp, cramp, blink

Analogy Charts

With Analogy Charts, students use the vowel patterns in words they know to help them write words they don't know. *Don't use Analogy Charts until students have mastered short vowels, digraphs, and blends.*

1. Use the Word Knowledge Inventory or your students' reading and spelling errors to identify two patterns to teach. If you teach the silent *e* feature, choose a short vowel pattern and long vowel pattern (e.g., *op* and *ope*). When teaching vowel clusters, choose two vowel patterns: one pattern students know fairly well and one new pattern (e.g., *ow* and *ea*). Common vowel patterns to teach are *ay, all, ar, or, ee, oo, er, ir, ur, ow, oa, ai, ea, ou, ew, oy, oi, aw, au, igh, eigh.*

2. Distribute an Analogy Chart Template (Appendix L) inserted in a plastic sheet protector, a dry-erase marker, and an eraser to each student.

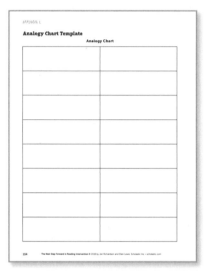

Appendix L and scholastic.com/ NSFIntervention

3. At the top of your chart, write two familiar words for each pattern (e.g., *hop* and *hope* or *cow* and *eat*). Have students copy those two words on their own charts and underline the vowel pattern in each one. Discuss the sound each pattern makes.

4. Tell students you are going to dictate new words for them to write. They should repeat the word and separate it into two parts. Model how to say the onset and rime (e.g., *cheat…ch-eat*). Say, *Listen to the vowel pattern and write the new word under the matching key word*. Then underline the pattern that's the same. Randomly dictate three or four words for each pattern. As students grow in proficiency, dictate words with inflectional endings, such as *cheater, eating,* and *slowly.*

5. Have students read the words in each column.

Chart 1 (top left): Description of Day 2

Begin with the easy analogies and gradually increase the difficulty of the task. Remember, these are examples, not a scope and sequence.

Easy Analogy Charts for Teaching Short and Long Vowels
(The rime and vowel sound don't change.)

cap	name	hit	like	hot	hope
clap	same	spit	bike	spot	rope
chap	shame	slit	hike	trot	slope
slap	blame	grit	spike	clot	scope
snap	flame	quit	strike	blot	grope

Easy Analogy Charts for Teaching Short and Long Vowels
(The rime and vowel sound don't change.)

run	cute	pin	dime	sick	line
fun	lute	thin	time	lick	vine
shun	mute	grin	slime	prick	twine
spun	flute	spin	grime	stick	shine
stun	brute	skin	crime	quick	spine

Harder Analogy Charts for Teaching Short and Long Vowels
(The rime changes but the vowel sound stays the same.)

cat	game	him	ride	hop	rode
chat	shake	chip	dike	shop	globe
mash	grape	spit	wife	spot	
brag	spade	crib	stripe	smog	
snap	scrape	slim	shine	glob	

THE NEXT STEP FORWARD IN GUIDED READING © 2016 by Jan Richardson, Scholastic Inc.

Transitional

Examples of Analogy Charts

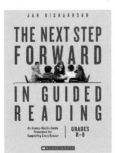

See pages 189 to 193 for examples of Analogy Charts.

Chart 2 (top right)

Harder Analogy Charts for Teaching Short and Long Vowels
(The rime changes but the vowel sound stays the same.)

fun	huge	hat	same	hot	note
stud	fume	chat	brake	spot	spoke
much	mule	champ	quake	drop	stone
brush	crude	last	grave	blog	drove
bump	tube	slam	whale	shock	quote

Hardest Analogy Charts for Teaching Short and Long Vowels
(Both the rime and vowel sound change.)

back (short)	cake (long)	did (short)	dime (long)	pot (short)	rope (long)
duck	trade	spot	broke	drag	drone
clock	pride	crab	spike	skip	frame
stick	chime	flip	smoke	slim	slime
quack	blame	squid	huge	scrap	scrape

Hardest Analogy Charts for Teaching Short and Long Vowels
(Both the rime and vowel sound change.)

sun (short)	name (long)	duck (short)	made (long)	cat (short)	ride (long)
duck	trade	slick	plane	chug	rule
				slid	slide
				strip	stripe
				smog	prune

THE NEXT STEP FORWARD IN GUIDED READING © 2016 by Jan Richardson, Scholastic Inc. • scholastic.com/NSFresources

Chart 3 (center bottom): Description of Day 2

Always choose patterns with two different sounds. Easier patterns are listed on the top rows.

Sample Analogy Charts for Teaching Vowel Patterns

day	ball	car	and	see	for
may	fall	far	sand	tree	fort
pray	small	card	stand	sweep	sport
stayed	smaller	started	branded	sleeping	stormy
spraying	tallest	harmful	stranded	sweeper	scorched

zoo	her	look	girl	eat	moon
shoot	germ	shook	bird	treat	pool
smooth	under	brook	third	dream	spoon
groom	over	stood	shirt	cheating	school
scooter	mother	crooked	firmly	teacher	snoopy

Transitional

THE NEXT STEP FORWARD IN GUIDED READING © 2016 by Jan Richardson, Scholastic Inc. • scholastic.com/NSFresources 191

RISE

Breaking Words

This activity, developed by Michele Dufresne, teaches students how to take words apart in reading. Use Breaking Words after you have introduced the target skill with Picture Sorting, Making Words, Sound Boxes, and Analogy Charts. When possible, link the target skill to your teaching point after reading. For example, if your teaching point is using *ay* to decode *stayed*, the Breaking Words activity would focus on other words that have the *ay* pattern.

Each student will need a tray of magnetic letters, a dry-erase board, and a marker. The teacher will need a dry-erase board and a marker.

PROCEDURES FOR BREAKING WORDS WITHOUT INFLECTIONAL ENDINGS (TEXT LEVELS E–I)

1. On a dry-erase board, the teacher writes a word that matches the word study focus. For example, at level E, you'll write a one-syllable word with an initial blend (*stop*). Do not say the word and do not have students say the word.

2. Have students remove the letters from their trays and make the word.

3. Tell students to break the word at the vowel (*st-op*). They should already be familiar with this action since they do it during the Making Words activity.

4. Have students say each part chorally (/st/ /op/).

5. Have them put the word back together and read it (*stop*).

6. Tell students to change one or two magnetic letters to make a new word. For example, you might say, *Change the letters "st" to "fl."* Do not say the word and do not have the students say the word. Repeat Steps 3, 4, and 5.

7. On a dry-erase board, write another word with the same rime but a different onset (e.g., *crop*). Have students read it. If they need help, underline the rime (*op*).

Examples of Words to Use at Each Text Level

Level	Focus	Examples
E	Initial blends and digraphs with simple rimes	crab (grab, scab, slab) black (shack, track, snack) sled (sped, fled, shred) chick (stick, brick, quick) swim (slim, trim, grim) frog (smog, clog, flog) shop (drop, flop, prop) plug (snug, drug, shrug) fly (dry, cry, sky)
F	Initial blends and digraphs with harder rimes	clamp (cramp, stamp, champ) stand (brand, grand, strand) blank (drank, crank, shrank) crash (smash, stash, flash) bless (dress, press, stress) print (glint, splint, squint) broom (bloom, gloom, groom) stung (swung, sprung, strung) skunk (stunk, trunk, shrunk)
G	Silent *e*	place (brace, grace, space) snake (brake, flake, quake) price (slice, twice, spice) chime (crime, grime, prime) swipe (gripe, snipe, stripe) broke (smoke, spoke, stroke) store (snore, shore, chore)
H–I	Complex vowels	stay (tray, stray, spray) chain (brain, grain, sprain) draw (claw, straw, squaw) speak (sneak, creak, squeak) dream (steam, scream, stream) bleed (breed, speed, freed) chew (blew, crew, threw) flight (fright, bright, slight) girl (swirl, twirl, whirl)

PROCEDURES FOR BREAKING WORDS WITH INFLECTIONAL ENDINGS (TEXT LEVELS G–L)

1. The teacher writes a word with an inflectional ending that matches the word study focus. For example, at level G, you would write a two-syllable word with a blend and an ending (e.g., *spinning*). Do not say the word and do not have students say the word.

2. Have students remove the letters from their trays and make the word. (You will need to provide double letters).

3. Tell students to move the ending to the right and break the word at the vowel (*sp-inn-ing*).

4. Have students say each part chorally (/sp/ /inn/ /ing/). Explain that you double the consonant when you add an ending to a word with a two-letter rime that has a short vowel (e.g., *at, ap, it, ip, op, un*).

5. Have students put the word back together and read it.

6. Have students use magnetic letters to change the onset or ending to make a new word (*spinning–grinning; spinning–spinner*). Do not say the word and do not have students say the word. Repeat Steps 3, 4, and 5 with the new word.

7. On a dry-erase board, write another word with the same rime but a different onset and/or ending (e.g., *thinner*). Have students read it. If they need help, underline the rime.

Examples of Words to Use at Each Text Level

Level	Focus	Examples
G–H	Simple rimes with inflectional endings (-ed, -ing, -er, -y, -le)	crabby (shabby, grabbed, scrabble) thinner (spinner, grinned, skinny) chatter (flatter, splatter, scatter) wedding (sledding, shredder, shredded) juggle (snuggle, smuggle, struggle) slammed (crammed, hammer, slamming) clapped (trapped, snapping, snappy) scamper (damper, clamping, cramped)
I–J	Vowel teams with inflectional endings (easier)	stayed (prayed, sprayer, straying) taller (smaller, stalled, smallest) starred (scarred, charred, starry) reached (bleached, teacher, preaching) dreamer (creamer, steaming, screamed) cheated (treated, meaty, heater) bleeding (speeding, greedy, needed) creepy (sleepy, sweeping, steeper)
K–L	Vowel teams with inflectional endings (harder)	hailing (nailing, mailed, trailer) drawing (clawing, gnawed, yawning) chewed (brewed, screwing, newly) cries (tries, spied, fried) tightly (brightly, frighten, mighty) floating (bloating, gloated, boasted) howling (prowling, growled, scowled)

Make a Big Word

This activity teaches students how to read and write multisyllabic words. Follow these procedures:

1. Select a multisyllabic word from the text. Choose a word that contains a phonetic principle students need to learn (e.g., -ly in *suddenly* and *secretly*).

2. Give each student the magnetic letters to make the word, or have them remove the needed letters from a magnetic letter tray.

3. Have students clap each syllable in the word and use the letters to construct each part.

4. Once they make the word correctly, have them break it into syllables, say each part, and then remake the word.

Make Spelling/Meaning Connections

Select a word from the text that can be connected to other words in meaningful ways. For example, you might select the word *submerge*, dictate it and other words that contain the feature *sub-* (e.g., *subject* and *subtract*), and have students write those words on a dry-erase board. Then briefly discuss the meaning of each word or use it in a sentence. See Appendix M for a list of common features and words that contain those features.

Students should leave the Phonics and Word Study Station having written three familiar sight words, learned a new sight word, worked with Magic Rimes, and practiced at least one meaningful word study activity that addresses their phonics needs.

RISE Station 2 Lesson Plan: Phonics and Word Study

Review known sight words, teach a new word, and do word study activities
to teach phonemic awareness and phonics skills.

Word Study Focus	Date
initial blends	11/3

Learn Sight Words (4–5 minutes)

Review three familiar words (writing):

you   come   said

Teach one new sight word: down

Do steps 1–4 in order:

1. What's Missing?
2. Mix and Fix
3. Table Writing
4. Write and Retrieve

Rime Magic for RISE: Step ___2___ (3–5 minutes)

Word Study Options (5–7 minutes)

☑ Picture Sorting   sl / sw

☑ Making Words   (g, i, m, n, s, t, w) in-win-twin, twig-swig-swim

☑ Sound Boxes   swim, slap, grub

☐ Analogy Charts

☑ Breaking Words   stick-slick-trick-brick

☐ Make a Big Word

☐ Make Spelling/Meaning Connections

Appendix B and scholastic.com/NSFIntervention

RISE Station 2 Lesson Plan: Phonics and Word Study

Record observations and next steps for individual students.

Name: Julian — needs to say words slowly	Name: Mia — wrote <u>sade</u> for <u>said</u>
Name: Daniel — good at breaking words	Name: Yaza — needed help with short vowels
Name: Soleana — good at beginning blends	Name: Sam — /sw/ was hard- speech issue
Name: Mariana — needs help with blends	Name: Mai — needs to say words slowly
Name: Adriel — review sight word for Level D	Name: Miriam — needs more work with digraphs
Name: Danya — Struggling with sight words. Needs more practice. Send magnetic letters home.	Name: Haset — Good at spelling sight words. Needs help with endings.
Name:	Name:
Name:	Name:

Notes From Daily Debriefing

Make sure students write some of the words during Rime Magic. Do more sound boxes to help students hear sounds in sequence. Work with some contractions, including <u>it's</u>.

Appendix B and scholastic.com/NSFIntervention

Station 3: Reread Yesterday's Book

The materials used at this station include the Story Retelling Rope (Appendix N), a Character Feelings and Traits Chart (Appendix Q), enlarged Comprehension Cards (Appendix R), and other reproducible and downloadable items, all found in the Appendices and at scholastic.com/NSFIntervention.

Begin by asking who read at home last night. Make a note to follow up if a student has not read at home more than two nights in a row. Speak to the student and contact the parent. We have found that after a week, students are so engaged in the RISE process that practice reading in school and at home is welcomed and very few need a reminder.

1. **Ask students to reread yesterday's new book.** Listen to each student read, and take notes in the boxes provided on the Reread Yesterday's Book Lesson Plan (Appendix C). Record miscues and self-corrections. Differentiate your prompting according to the needs of the student.

See pages 125 and 178 for additional prompts that help students take risks, monitor for meaning and visual information, solve words, read with fluency, and check for comprehension.

(handwritten, left margin) Improve Comprehension

2. **After students read the book, lead a discussion based on the comprehension needs of the group.** Use the anecdotal notes you took during the lesson to identify a few strategies to improve their comprehension. Match the strategies to one or more of the following discussion starters.

- **Beginning-Middle-End (B-M-E) card.** Direct students' attention to the enlarged B-M-E card. Students take turns telling one part of the story. Encourage students to include as many details as they can when it is their turn to talk.

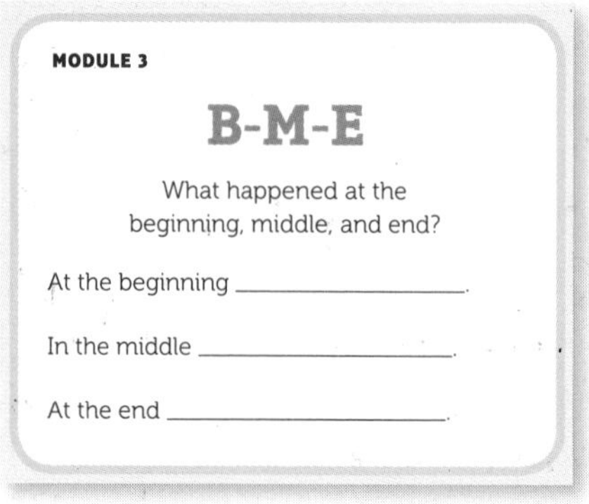

(handwritten, right) Details

> MODULE 3
>
> ## B-M-E
>
> What happened at the beginning, middle, and end?
>
> At the beginning _____.
>
> In the middle _____.
>
> At the end _____.

Appendix R and scholastic.com/ NSFIntervention

- **Connections.** Invite students to share their connections with the book. Ask if this book reminds them of something they have done or another book they have read.

- **Problem-Solution card.** Direct students' attention to the enlarged Problem-Solution card. Discuss the problem and solution, and record key words for each one.

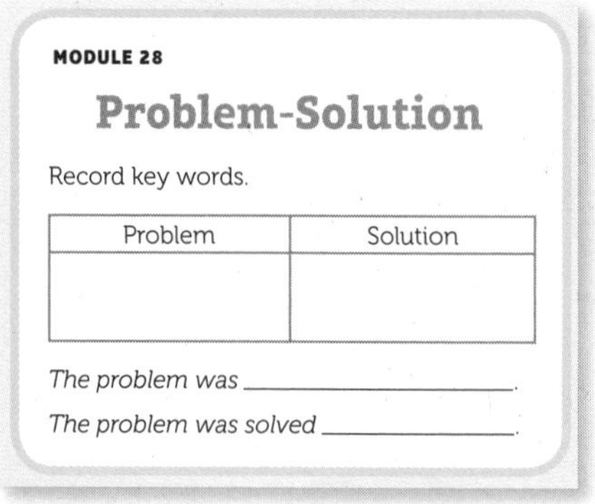

> MODULE 28
>
> ## Problem-Solution
>
> Record key words.
>
> | Problem | Solution |
> |---------|----------|
> | | |
>
> *The problem was* _____.
>
> *The problem was solved* _____.

Appendix R and scholastic.com/ NSFIntervention

- **Story Retelling Rope.** This scaffold helps students retell story elements.

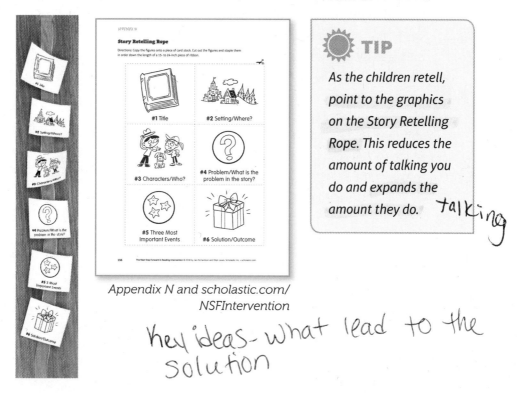

Appendix N and scholastic.com/ NSFIntervention

Appendix N and scholastic.com/ NSFIntervention

TIP

As the children retell, point to the graphics on the Story Retelling Rope. This reduces the amount of talking you do and expands the amount they do. talking

Key ideas- what lead to the solution

- **Shared Retelling Cards.** Give each student a Shared Retelling Card and guide them as they take turns retelling a portion of the book.

Sequence (sticky notes)

Shared Retelling Cards APPENDIX O

In the beginning...	Next...
The problem is...	After that...
Then...	Finally...

The Next Step Forward in Reading Intervention © 2018 by Jan Richardson and Ellen Lewis. Scholastic Inc. • scholastic.com   157

Appendix O and scholastic.com/ NSFIntervention

Appendix O and scholastic.com/ NSFIntervention

TIP

On sticky notes, write a key word or phrase to identify important events. Then randomly give each child a sticky note. After the children sequence the sticky notes, have them do a shared retelling.

RISE

- **Somebody-Wanted-But-So (SWBS) card.** Direct students' attention to the enlarged SWBS card. Ask students who the "Somebody" is. Write the main character's name on the board. Then ask, *What did the character want?* Write this next to the character's name. Have students tell you the problem (but), and how the problem was solved (so), as you write their ideas down.

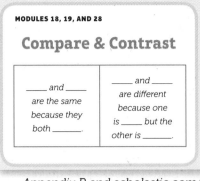

MODULE 24

SWBS

_____ wanted _____
(somebody)

but _____ so _____ .

Then _____ .

Appendix R and scholastic.com/ NSFIntervention

- **Green and Red Questions cards.** Direct students' attention to one of the enlarged question cards. Invite them to ask a question that begins with the card's starter. Pair up students to ask and answer questions.

MODULE 8

Green Questions

I must go to the text and find the answer.

Who . . . ?	When . . . ?
What . . . ?	How . . . ?
Where . . . ?	Which . . . ?

MODULE 9

Red Questions

I must stop and think about the answer.

Why . . . ?

Why do you think . . . ?

How . . . ?

What if . . . ?

Appendix R and scholastic.com/ NSFIntervention

- **Compare & Contrast card.** Direct students' attention to the enlarged Compare & Contrast card. Ask students to find two characters or concepts in the book that are similar or different. Discuss their similarities and differences. For example, discuss how flies and bees are similar and different. How is the character in this story similar to (or different from) the character in another story we've read?

MODULES 18, 19, AND 28

Compare & Contrast

____ and ____ are the same because they both ____ .	____ and ____ are different because one is ____ but the other is ____ .

Appendix R and scholastic.com/ NSFIntervention

- **Character Feelings and Traits Charts.** Use these charts to help students think of words that describe the characters in the story. Encourage them to use words other than *happy*, *glad*, *sad*, and *mad*. Explain the meaning of unfamiliar words, and prompt them to use those words as they talk about the characters.

Character Feelings and Traits Charts (Levels C–I)

Feeling: How does the character feel now? **Trait:** How does the character act most of the time?

Happy	Sad	Mad	Good
glad	unhappy	angry	kind
joyful	sorry	upset	helpful
proud	hurt	cross	safe
merry	gloomy	grumpy	friendly
thrilled	lonely	grouchy	thankful
pleasant	hopeless	moody	caring
excited	ashamed	cranky	polite

Scared	Mean	Brave	Other
afraid	selfish	unafraid	lazy
frightened	rude	bold	clever
nervous	cruel	fearless	hopeful
shy	greedy	daring	bored
worried	nasty	confident	curious

Appendix Q and scholastic.com/NSFIntervention

> ☀ **TIP**
>
> *When discussing story characters, if the children use an everyday word, such as* happy, mad, *or* sad, *have them refer to the Character Feelings and Traits Charts to find better, more precise words.*

- **Very Important Part (V.I.P.) Fiction card.** Direct students' attention to the enlarged V.I.P. Fiction card and review the steps. Then have them find a page in the book that includes an important event. This is a "very important part" of the story. The most important event in a story often reveals the central message or theme.

At the end of the session, share your notes with the other RISE instructors, pick the next book students will read, and plan the focus for the next day's lesson.

MODULE 10

V.I.P.
Fiction

Action—What is the most important thing the character did?

Feeling—What is the most important feeling the character had?

Appendix R and scholastic.com/NSFIntervention

▶ **VIDEO LINK**
Station 3: Reread Yesterday's Book

RISE Station 3 Lesson Plan: Reread Yesterday's Book

Reread and discuss yesterday's book.

Book Title	Level	Date
Is This a Real Animal?	E	11/3

Comprehension Focus

Compare & Contrast

Monitoring and Word-Solving Prompts

☑ (Are you right?) Does it make sense? Does it look right?

☑ Reread and sound the first part.

☐ What would make sense and look right?

☐ Check the middle (or end) of the word.

☐ Cover the ending. Find a part you know.

☐ Do you know another word that looks like this one?

☐ Try the other vowel sound.

☐ Use a known part.

☑ Look all the way to the end of the word.
      contraction [It's]

See *The Next Step Forward in Guided Reading*, pages 125 and 178, for additional prompts.

Fluency Prompts

☑ (Don't point.) Read it faster.

☐ Read it the way the character would say it.

☐ I'll frame the words. You read them together.

☑ Attend to punctuation.

Comprehension Discussion Starters

☐ Beginning-Middle-End (B-M-E)

☐ Connections

☐ Problem-Solution

☐ Story Retelling Rope

☐ Shared Retelling

☐ Somebody-Wanted-But-So (SWBS)

☐ Green Questions

☐ Red Questions

☑ Compare & Contrast   How are these two similar? Different? Find two animals that are different; similar.

☐ Character Feelings and Traits

☐ Very Important Part (V.I.P.)

Appendix C and scholastic.com/NSFIntervention

RISE Station 3 Lesson Plan: Reread Yesterday's Book

Record observations and next steps for individual students.	
Name: Miriam ✓✓ $\dfrac{\text{It is}}{\text{It's}}$ ✓✓ Prompt for punctuation	**Name:** Mia ✓✓✓ $\overline{\text{real}}$ ✓✓ ✓✓✓✓✓✓ ✓✓ Prompt for monitoring
Name: Mai ✓✓✓ ✓ learning to compare/contrast Prompt to engage in discussion	**Name:** Yaza ✓✓✓✓✓✓ ✓✓✓✓ strong with compare/contrast Prompt for punctuation
Name: Haset ✓✓✓✓+decoding Prompt for punctuation	**Name:** Sam ✓✓✓✓✓✓✓ ✓✓✓✓✓✓✓ $\dfrac{\text{lot}}{\text{lots}}$ ✓ $\dfrac{\text{lot}}{\text{lots}}$ ✓✓✓ Prompt for endings
Name: Julian ✓✓✓✓✓✓✓ Prompt to slow down ✓✓✓ $\dfrac{\text{it's}}{\text{it is}}$ ✓✓✓✓	**Name:** Mariana ✓✓✓✓✓ ✓✓✓ $\dfrac{\text{It's}}{\text{It is}}$ ✓✓✓✓ Prompt for fluency
Name: Daniel ✓✓✓✓✓ ✓✓✓✓✓✓ $\dfrac{\text{jumped}}{\text{just}}$ ✓✓✓ Prompt for monitoring	**Name:** Adriel ✓✓✓✓✓ ✓✓✓✓ accurate, fluent ✓✓ Prompt for deeper comprehension
Name: Soleana ✓✓✓✓✓✓✓ ✓✓ $\dfrac{\text{the}}{\text{a}}$ ✓✓✓	**Name:** Danya ✓✓✓✓✓✓✓ ✓✓✓✓ $\dfrac{\text{look}}{\text{like}}$ Prompt for expression ✓✓ — punctuation
Name:	**Name:**
Name:	**Name:**

Notes From Daily Debriefing

Attend to punctuation.
Focus on phrasing and expression.

Appendix C and scholastic.com/NSFIntervention

RISE

Station 4: Guided Writing

Students spend about 15 minutes writing about yesterday's new book. Guided writing extends comprehension and improves writing skills because you are coaching students as they write.

Most students will have reread the book in Station 3 before they come to the Guided Writing Station. Students whose first station is Guided Writing, however, will not have read the book that day. RISE works best if the strongest readers are scheduled to visit the Guided Writing Station first because they have a better chance of remembering what they read the day before.

☀ **TIP**

The materials needed for this station include a writing journal and pencil for each student. You can make journals using templates in Appendix P and at scholastic.com/ NSFIntervention and following these directions.

For each journal, make 20 two-sided pages. Invert the text for the back side of the page. Add a cover made with heavier card stock. Fold and staple in the middle of the journal.

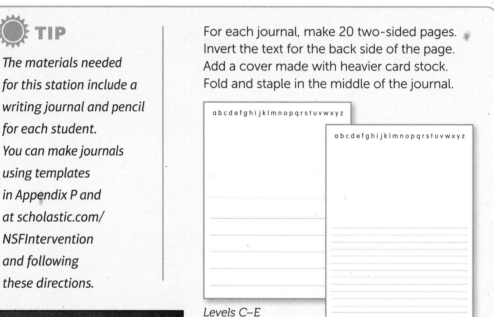

Levels C–E

Levels F–I

For each journal, make 20 two-sided pages. Maintain the same orientation on the back side. Add a cover of heavier stock. Fold and staple.

Levels J–N

The Next Step Forward in Reading Intervention © 2018 by Jan Richardson and Ellen Lewis. Published by Scholastic Inc.

Follow these steps:

1. Dictate one sentence about the beginning of the book. Include sight words the students are learning and a word or two that will help them apply the target skill addressed at the Phonics and Word Study Station. This is an opportunity to create echoes across the stations. For example, if students sorted pictures with short *a* and *o* in word study, you would want to include some words with these vowel sounds in the dictated sentence. We have found that dictating the first sentence gets the students writing quickly so they don't waste time.

2. Work with individual students who need help. Prompt them to say words slowly so they can hear sounds, correctly spell sight words they have been taught, use correct letter formation, and reread the sentence to determine the next word to write. Encourage students to sound out unfamiliar words, and celebrate invented spelling.

3. After students complete the dictated sentence, prompt them to write more about the book. The Guided Writing Lesson Plan (Appendix D) lists several response options. When appropriate, give students one of the Comprehension Cards used at the Reread Yesterday's Book Station. The card will support students as they put their own ideas on paper. You might also give them a personal word wall to use as a spelling resource (Appendix S).

4. As students progress, raise your expectations for their writing. Use the following charts (pages 54 to 60) to guide your instruction. At the lower levels, dictate the sentences. Include the new sight word, familiar words, and the phonics skill taught that week at the Phonics and Word Study Station. When students reach text level G, discontinue dictated sentences and shift to student-generated responses. You may still need to guide the students as they compose their own ideas.

   Some students reading at higher text levels (especially those learning English) may still need a dictated sentence to help them get started. Use an open-ended sentence that includes the structure for the response. For example, if students are writing a comparison, you might dictate, *Charlie and Jodie are similar in several ways. They were both....*

VIDEO LINK

Station 4: Guided Writing

Guided Writing Expectations by Text Level

The following charts will guide you as you make on-the-spot decisions about what to expect and what to teach during guided writing. Your expectations should change as children move up in text levels.

Level C

Format: One or two dictated sentences of seven to ten words. Draw a line for each word.

Target Skills	
With prompting	**Without prompting**
Spell new sight words correctly.	Repeat the sentence.
Record short *e*, *i*, and *u*.	Say each word while writing it.
Practice correct letter formation.	Hear and record easy-to-hear consonants.
Use periods.	Record long vowels.
Reread the sentence.	Record short *a* and *o*.
Say words slowly to hear sounds.	Spell familiar sight words correctly.
	Space words with the help of teacher-drawn lines.

Level D

Format: Two (or more) dictated sentences of seven to ten words.

Target Skills	
With prompting	**Without prompting**
Spell new sight words correctly.	Reread the sentence.
Use periods and capital letters.	Say words slowly to hear sounds.
Form letters that touch the line.	Record all consonants and long vowels.
Record digraphs.	Record all medial vowels.
Use lowercase letters correctly.	Put spaces between words.
Add endings to known words (-*ing*, -*s*).	Spell familiar sight words correctly.
Use correct letter formation.	

TIP

After students write the dictated sentences, prompt them to add sentences. They can tell how the character felt at the end of the story or describe one of the illustrations.

Level E

Format: One dictated sentence of seven to ten words. Additional sentences constructed by the student.

Target Skills	
With prompting	**Without prompting**
Spell new sight words correctly.	Reread the sentence.
Rehearse each sentence to hear the period.	Say words slowly to hear sounds.
Use a capital letter at the beginning of each sentence.	Spell unknown words phonetically.
Form letters that drop below line. (g, j, p, y)	Record digraphs and vowels.
Record initial blends.	Add endings to known words (-s, -ing).
Use handwriting paper.	Use lowercase letters correctly.
Capitalize proper names.	Put spaces between words.
Add -ed to known words.	Spell familiar sight words correctly.
	Use periods.

 The Next Step Forward in Reading Intervention © 2018 by Jan Richardson and Ellen Lewis. Published by Scholastic Inc.

Level F

Format: One dictated sentence of seven to ten words. Additional sentences constructed by the student.

Target Skills	
With prompting	**Without prompting**
Spell new sight words correctly.	Reread the sentence to remember next word.
Record final blends.	Say words slowly while writing.
Use handwriting paper.	Spell unknown words phonetically.
Capitalize proper names.	Record digraphs and initial blends.
Compose a beginning, middle, and end.	Add endings to known words (-ing, -s, -ed).
Write known parts in words (e.g., to-day).	Use lowercase letters correctly.
Use question marks.	Put spaces between words.
Reread the sentence to check for accuracy.	Spell familiar sight words correctly.
Use exclamation marks.	Use a capital letter at the beginning of a sentence.
Add -er to known words.	Remember the period at the end of a sentence.

Level G/H

Format: Several student-generated sentences in response to the teacher's prompt.

Target Skills	
With prompting	**Without prompting**
Spell new sight words correctly.	Reread the sentence to check accuracy.
Compose a SWBS.	Spell unknown words phonetically.
Write a two-syllable word phonetically.	Record digraphs and blends.
Apply the silent *e* feature.	Use upper- and lowercase letters correctly.
Compose a beginning, middle, and end, using key words.	Use handwriting paper.
Write about a text feature.	Add endings to known words (-*ed*, -*er*).
Use a familiar word to write a new word.	Use periods and exclamation marks correctly.
Add -*ly* to known words.	Write known parts in words.

 TIP

Some emerging bilingual students will need you to dictate the first sentence. This helps them use language structures appropriately and gets them started with writing.

Level I/J/K

Format: Several student-generated sentences in response to the teacher's prompt.

Target Skills	
With prompting	**Without prompting**
Spell new sight words correctly.	Reread the sentence to check accuracy.
Write about a character's feelings.	Add endings to known words (-*ly*, -*er*).
Use a word wall to check spelling.	Spell familiar sight words.
Write a retelling.	Use handwriting paper.
Use a familiar word to write a new word.	Use periods and capital letters correctly.
Apply the silent *e* feature.	Write known parts in words (e.g., *to-day*).
Use the book as a spelling resource.	Compose a SWBS.
Add endings to known words (-*y*,-*ful*, -*est*).	Compose a beginning, middle, and end, using key words.
Apply vowel patterns you have taught.	Write about a text feature.
Use transition words at the beginning of some sentences (*first, after that, then, next, finally*).	Use a familiar word to write a new word.
	Write a two-syllable word phonetically.

Level L/M/N

Format: Several student-generated sentences in response to the teacher's prompt.

Target Skills	
With prompting	**Without prompting**
Write a three-syllable word phonetically.	Use a personal word wall as a spelling resource (Appendix S and scholastic.com/NSFIntervention).
Apply vowel patterns you have taught.	Reread the sentence to check accuracy.
Drop the silent *e* when adding *-ing*.	Write a two-syllable word phonetically.
Double the final consonant when adding *-ing* (*running, stopping*).	Spell unfamiliar words phonetically.
Add details about the topic.	Add endings to known words (*-y, -ful, -est*).
Include dialogue to provide text evidence.	Apply the silent *e* feature.
Use quotation marks when writing dialogue.	Use lowercase letters correctly.
Write about a character's feelings.	Use handwriting paper.
Compose steps to a procedure.	Spell familiar sight words.
Write questions about the text.	Use end punctuation and capital letters.
Write a retelling.	Write known parts in words (e.g., *to-day*).
Spell common prefixes and suffixes correctly.	Compose a SWBS.
Combine sentences and use introductory clauses that begin with *although, while, after, during, since, later,* etc.	Compose a beginning, middle, and end, using key words.

 The Next Step Forward in Reading Intervention © 2018 by Jan Richardson and Ellen Lewis. Published by Scholastic Inc.

RISE Station 4 Lesson Plan: Guided Writing

Write about yesterday's new book.

Book Title	Level	Date
Is This a Real Animal?	E	11/3

Dictated Sentences or Writing Prompt

The big fish is <u>down</u> in the water. (New sight word: down)
(Students write 1–2 sentences of their own.)
The _____ has _____.

Guided Writing Response Options for Levels E–N

☐ Beginning-Middle-End (B-M-E)

☐ Problem-Solution

☑ New Facts You Learned

☐ Somebody-Wanted-But-So (SWBS)

☐ Track a Character's Feelings

☐ Describe a Character's Traits

☐ V.I.P. (Very Important Part of the Story)

☐ Compare & Contrast

☐ Five-Finger Retell

☐ Write Questions and Answer Them

☐ Other:

Plan for Writing
(List key words or create graphic organizer.)

cat, dog, mole

Target Skills
(List skills to teach today.)
- Say words slowly
- Use a period at the end of each sentence
- Reread to remember the sentence

Appendix D and scholastic.com/NSFIntervention

RISE Station 4 Lesson Plan: Guided Writing

Record observations and next steps for individual students.	
Name: Mariana ✓ ✓ ✓ ✓ $\frac{donw}{down}$ ✓ ✓ $\frac{wotr}{water}$	Name: Julian ✓ ✓ ✓ $\frac{—}{big}$ ✓ ✓ ✓ ✓ $\frac{}{water}$
Name: Adriel ✓ ✓ ✓ ✓ ✓ ✓ $\frac{wotr}{water}$ mixture of upper/lowercase letters	Name: Daniel $\frac{wotr}{mole}$ ✓ ✓ ✓ ✓ ✓ ✓ mole $\frac{nos}{nose}$ The mole has a nose
Name: Danya ✓ ✓ ✓ ✓ ✓ ✓ ✓ ✓ ✓ ✓ ✓ ✓ ✓ The shark has big teeth	Name: Soleana ✓ ✓ ✓ ✓ prompted for a capital letter.
Name: Miriam ✓ ✓ ✓ ✓ ✓ ✓ ✓ $\frac{wtr}{water}$	Name: Mia ✓ ✓ ✓ ✓ ✓ ✓ ✓ $\frac{wotr}{water}$ periods.
Name: Mai ✓ ✓ ✓ ✓ ✓ ✓ ✓ $\frac{wodr}{water}$ Prompted for a period.	Name: Yaza ✓ $\frac{beg}{big}$ ✓ $\frac{don}{down}$ ✓ ✓ $\frac{wotr}{water}$
Name: Haset ✓ ✓ ✓ ✓ ✓ ✓ ✓ ✓ letter formation d	Name: Sam — used boxes ✓ ✓ $\frac{fi}{fish}$ ✓ $\frac{don}{down}$ ✓ water (boxed)
Name:	Name:
Name:	Name:

Notes From Daily Debriefing

Incorporate some simple contractions in the dictated sentence.
Work on letter formation (b, d).

Appendix D and scholastic.com/NSFIntervention

TEAM MEETINGS AND LESSON PLANNING

After the children return to class, the instructors meet for about five minutes to share their observations, teaching points, and concerns. This collaboration helps them monitor progress, celebrate successes, and plan the next day's RISE lesson. The instructors of Stations 1, 2, and 3 should explain the skills they taught so that the Guided Writing instructor can plan to have students practice them. If the reading teacher noticed students ignoring inflectional endings, the Phonics and Word Study instructor could focus on Making and Breaking Words with such endings. The Guided Writing instructor could encourage students to say each word slowly and record the ending. The instructor at the Reread Yesterday's Book Station could prompt students to look all the way to the end of the word.

The daily opportunity to reflect on the lesson and make decisions about the next lesson is one of the many strengths of RISE. To make the most of the 12 to 15 minutes at each station, instructors need to identify specific teaching goals for each lesson and record the goals on their lesson plans.

▶ **VIDEO LINK**

RISE Team Meeting

Monitoring Progress

The New Book teacher carefully monitors student progress by taking daily mini-records. Those records, coupled with a formal running record taken every three to four weeks, help the team decide when students are ready to exit the intervention and return to classroom guided reading instruction.

 TIP

Use charts such as this one to track attendance and growth. The dot indicates the child was present that day. A different color dot is used to indicate the group moved up a text level.

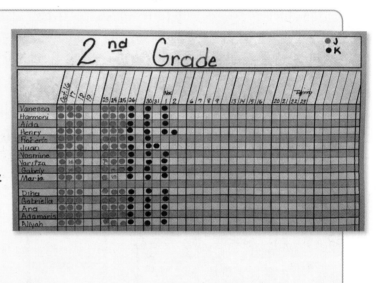

Connecting With Classroom Teachers

Because RISE lessons are the primary form of guided reading instruction these students receive during the intervention period, the team should meet weekly with the classroom teachers to update them on student progress.

At the end of the eight-week intervention, administer a formal assessment, such as *Next Step Guided Reading Assessment* (Richardson & Walther, 2013), *Developmental Reading Assessment* (Beaver, 2012), or *Benchmark Assessment System* (Fountas & Pinnell, 2016), and write a short summary of progress on each student for the classroom teacher. Suggest strategies to emphasize in guided reading lessons. (See sample on the next page.)

Our research based on field-testing indicates that the average rate of acceleration is one text level every two to two-and-a-half weeks. The majority of RISE students exit the intervention as confident and competent readers who continue to accelerate. The next chapter will guide you in creating a smooth and successful implementation.

RISE: End-of-Program Report

Student	Entry Level	Exit Level	# of Lessons	Notes for Classroom Teachers
Benjamin	D	I	36	**READING:** Strong decoder. Monitors, self-corrects, uses information systems to solve words. Makes predictions, connections, and inferences. Identifies character traits. **WRITING:** Writes complete sentences. Has increased sight word vocabulary. **RECOMMENDATIONS:** Provide practice with retelling. Continue to review and teach sight words. Move to level J.
Imran	C	I	40	**READING:** Strong decoder but inserts or omits words and endings. Self-prompts and notices when the text doesn't make sense. Good comprehension. **WRITING:** Needs to reread and check for words he has omitted. **RECOMMENDATIONS:** Needs to work on silent *e* feature and vowel teams. Encourage him to slow down when reading and writing to monitor, reread, and self-correct. Use the STP strategy on short texts. Ask Green and Red Questions to improve literal and deeper comprehension. Move to level J.
Dayanna	C	I	38	**READING:** Strong decoder. Notices errors, self-monitors, and self-corrects. Uses all information systems to problem-solve unknown words. Reads with expression. Good with sequencing events. **WRITING:** Generates ideas without support. Good visual memory. Large bank of known sight words. **RECOMMENDATIONS:** Use Green and Red Questions and STP to improve comprehension. Move to level J.
Ivan	D	I	38	**READING:** Enthusiastic reader. Good decoder and risk-taker. Uses information systems to solve words. Attends to endings most of the time, but he needs some prompting. Needs to add details to his retellings. **WRITING:** Writing is his strength. Focused and organized. Good mechanics. **RECOMMENDATIONS:** Work on retelling. Encourage conversations to improve oral language. Work on verb tenses and attending to endings. Move to level J.
Yonatan	C	I	40	**READING:** Strong decoder but needs help staying on task. Monitors with prompting. Tends to copy others when reading and writing. When the text is interesting to him, he can predict and use character traits. Struggles with retelling. **WRITING:** Yonatan is reluctant to write because he struggles with spelling. Have him use the personal word wall as a spelling resource. **RECOMMENDATIONS:** Work on monitoring and completing tasks. Stay at level I for two more weeks.
Labib	C	I	40	**READING:** Still learning to understand English language structures. Weak vocabulary. Works hard and stays on task. Uses meaning and visual information, but neglects structure when reading and writing. Enjoys reading nonfiction texts. Decodes slowly, but is beginning to take words apart. Monitors for meaning but struggles with endings. Has high expectations for himself and a desire to succeed. **WRITING:** Follows instruction and applies it to his work. Works hard on spelling words correctly and including word endings. May need scaffolding to get started. Have him tell you his sentence before he writes it. **RECOMMENDATIONS:** Work on fluency (buddy reading, readers' theater, rereading familiar books). Stay at level I for a week to improve fluency, then move to J.

CHAPTER 3

RISE in Action

RISE calls for partnering with a team of stakeholders—the principal, classroom teachers, reading teachers, specialists, intervention teachers, and parents. The first thing to do is meet with the stakeholders to explain the program. Emphasize that RISE is an intensive, short-term intervention that quickly accelerates up to 16 striving readers at a time in six to eight weeks. Be sure to explain how the four rotations are an extended version of the lesson framework in *The Next Step Forward in Guided Reading* (Richardson, 2016). You can use the PowerPoint and videos provided on the resource website (scholastic.com/NSFIntervention) during this orientation meeting. If RISE is implemented near the beginning of the school year, it is possible to teach four rounds of RISE with different groups of students. In other words, 48 to 64 students can be accelerated in one year by doing one hour of RISE each day!

PREPARING FOR RISE

As you implement this intervention, be sure to address all the topics described in this section.

Schedule a Time

Ask the administrators and classroom teachers to designate one hour every day for RISE. It works best if the RISE hour occurs during the grade-level language arts block so students do not miss out on classroom instruction in other content areas. However, RISE can be taught at any time of the day. Several schools have opted to use their intervention hour or extended day program.

Locate a Space

Find a room large enough to accommodate up to 16 students, four instructors, and four stations. If space is limited, consider using the cafeteria or any other room that is vacant one hour a day.

Station 1: Read a New Book

Station 2: Phonics and Word Study

Station 3: Reread Yesterday's Book

Station 4: Guided Writing

Train the Instructors

Identify people who are available one hour a day to teach this intervention. The RISE leader should be a credentialed teacher who has a good understanding of the reading process and is familiar with *The Next Step Forward in Guided Reading* lesson components. He or she will train the other members of the team, monitor student progress, communicate with classroom teachers, and assist with lesson planning. The other instructors can be specialists, teaching assistants, student teachers, retired teachers, and other adults who routinely work with students in your school.

Gather Materials

Because students will be reading a new book every day, you will need a set of books ranging from levels C–N. It's important for students to take home easy books they can read with a parent. If you have enough copies, send a book home with each student. If you don't, allow students to select books from your leveled book room or classroom library to read at home. Because those books are likely to be unfamiliar, children should choose ones that are below the text level they read in RISE.

Each instructor needs blank lesson plans (Appendices A–D) and a tabletop easel or dry-erase board. Also gather and organize the instructional materials for each station. See the following chart.

If the RISE instructors are not familiar with the lesson procedures for early and transitional guided reading, do a study of Chapters 4 and 5. Show the videos for each lesson component, and have teachers practice by role-playing the part of the teacher and student. Be sure that instructors understand the purposes and procedures for each station. Plan several lessons together.

Instructional Materials for Each Station

Station 1:
Read a New Book

- Multiple copies of a new book (1 per student)
- Sticky notes and flags
- Story Retelling Rope (Appendix N and scholastic.com/NSFIntervention)
- Shared Retelling Cards (Appendix O and scholastic.com/NSFIntervention)
- Word-Solving Strategies Card (Appendix T and scholastic.com/NSFIntervention)

Station 2:
Phonics and Word Study

- 4 dry-erase boards and markers
- 4 trays of magnetic letters
- 4 Sound Box Templates in plastic sleeves (Appendix K and scholastic.com/NSFIntervention)
- 4 Analogy Chart Templates in plastic sleeves (Appendix L and scholastic.com/NSFIntervention)
- Pictures for sorting medial vowels, digraphs, and initial blends
- Rime Magic for RISE cards (Appendix J and scholastic.com/NSFIntervention)

Station 3:
Reread Yesterday's Book

- Multiple copies of yesterday's Station 1 book
- 4 Character Feelings and Traits Charts (Appendix Q and scholastic.com/NSFIntervention)
- 6 8-x-11 Comprehension Cards (Appendix R and scholastic.com/NSFIntervention)
- Story Retelling Rope (Appendix N and scholastic.com/NSFIntervention)
- Shared Retelling Cards (Appendix O and scholastic.com/NSFIntervention)
- Word-Solving Strategies Card (Appendix T and scholastic.com/NSFIntervention)

Station 4:
Guided Writing

- Multiple copies of yesterday's Station 1 book
- Writing journals (1 per student) (Appendix P and scholastic.com/NSFIntervention)
- Pencils
- 4 Personal Word Walls (Appendix S and scholastic.com/NSFIntervention)

Assess the Students

Determine which assessments you will use to select RISE students. Although most leveled reading assessments can help you identify students who need reading intervention, we recommend using *Next Step Guided Reading Assessment* (Richardson & Walther, 2013), *Developmental Reading Assessment* (Beaver, 2012), or *Benchmark Assessment System* (Fountas & Pinnell, 2016). We like them because they include a running record to help identify processing strengths and needs. Record each student's instructional level on a data chart, which will help you select students for RISE.

Select a RISE Group

Choose students who are reading at the same text-level range (no more than one level apart). Divide them into four groups so they can rotate through the stations. To allow for personalized and targeted instruction, keep the groups small, no more than four students. If you do RISE near the beginning of the year with first graders, select students reading at text level C. Students reading below level C do not have the stamina to endure a 45- to 60-minute intervention.

Place students reading at text levels A or B in an alternative intervention for a few weeks until they know about 15 to 20 sight words and are proficient with one-to-one matching and using picture clues. We suggest that they receive a guided reading lesson from their classroom teacher for 20 minutes each day and a second guided reading lesson later in the day with a reading teacher or interventionist. Consider them for RISE as soon as they are reading at text level C and have the stamina to endure a 45- to 60-minute lesson.

RISE 1: 1st Grade, Winter, Begins Jan. 22

Student	Instructional Reading Level	Teacher	Group
Zalan	D	Soderstrom	3
Daniel	D	McColl	1
Juliette	D	Soderstrom	4
Landon	D	Soderstrom	4
Dylan	D	McColl	2
Katherine	D	McColl	2
Victoria	D	McColl	1
Santiago	D	McColl	2
Dylan	C	Soderstrom	1
Cristian	C	Soderstrom	3
Camila	C	Soderstrom	3
Sady	D	McColl	4

RISE student roster

After you select your group, assess students using the Sight Word Charts for Monitoring Progress (Appendix G) and the Word Knowledge Inventory (Appendix H). Results from these two tools will guide instruction at the Phonics and Word Study and Guided Writing Stations. Administer the Sight Word Assessment to see which words your students can write. It is quick, easy, and useful. Dictate the words for their instructional text level and one level below and have students write them. On the Sight Word Chart, place a check mark next to known words for each student.

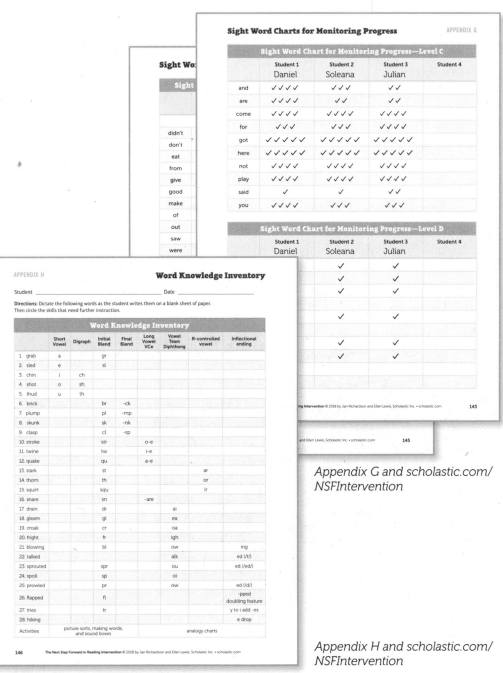

Appendix G and scholastic.com/NSFIntervention

Appendix H and scholastic.com/NSFIntervention

You can use the Word Knowledge Inventory to identify phonics skills that need to be taught. Administer the assessment like a spelling test and circle the phonics skills children miss. Teach those skills at the Phonics and Word Study Station.

Throughout the intervention, watch for students who are lagging behind, and intervene before they become frustrated. Meet with your RISE team and the classroom teachers to discuss why the student isn't progressing. Ask the following questions.

- Are we choosing appropriate books?

- Are we praising for partially correct answers?

- Are we planning word study activities that teach the skills the student needs to learn?

- Is the student reading at home?

- Does the student come to school every day?

Analyze the student's reading and writing behaviors to identify why he or she struggles. Try some of the following procedures on page 73, and share them with the classroom teachers.

For RISE to go smoothly, students must be reading at about the same text level so that instructors can repeat the lesson four times without needing to create a new plan for each rotating group. In the unlikely event that a student can't keep up with the rest of the group, he or she should take a break from RISE and be given an additional daily guided reading lesson at his or her instructional level. The student can then re-enter RISE in a few weeks.

For additional information on analyzing problem areas for students who are not accelerating, see pages 95 to 98, 147 to 152, and 203 to 214.

 The Next Step Forward in Reading Intervention © 2018 by Jan Richardson and Ellen Lewis. Published by Scholastic Inc.

If...	Then...
the student is afraid to take risks...	• say, *Try it. Sound the first part and check your picture.* • after any attempt, praise the student. *I like the way you tried that.* • ignore miscues until the student begins to attempt unknown words.
the student lacks fluency...	• assign easy books to read at home and in the classroom. • find an older student who can listen to the RISE student read familiar books for 15 minutes a day before or after school. • emphasize to the parent the importance of having the child read at home every night.
the student is not remembering sight words...	• every Monday, send home a set of magnetic letters and a list of five to eight sight words for the student to practice throughout the week. They should be words you have taught during the lessons the week before. Ask a parent to dictate each word and have the student make it with magnetic letters and then write it.
the student is not monitoring for meaning...	• ask, *Are you right? Does that make sense?* • prompt the student to use the picture, reread the sentence, and think what would make sense.
the student has trouble decoding...	• teach and prompt for word-solving actions, such as sound the first part, think about the story, check the end of the word, find a part you know, cover the ending, or use a known word to make an analogy.

IMPLEMENTING RISE

Before you begin instruction, meet with students to explain the intervention, introduce the materials, and teach routines and procedures.

Orientation Day

Bring the students to the RISE room for about 30 minutes of orientation. Explain that they have been chosen to come to RISE every day so they can become better readers and writers. Organize students into four groups and direct each group to one of the stations. Students will spend about five minutes at each station to learn procedures, work with materials, and practice routines. After five minutes, ring a chime or bell and have them move to the next station. Repeat the rotations until students have visited all four stations and practiced the routines. This would be a great time to do some cheerleading. Encourage the kids to work hard and never give up—and tell them how lucky they are to be selected for this program.

Set Up for Orientation Day

At the Read a New Book Station, children should see engaging, leveled books waiting on the table. The Phonics and Word Study Station should have magnetic letters, dry-erase markers, small dry-erase boards, Sound Boxes, Analogy Charts, and the rime cards. The Reread Yesterday's Book Station should have a set of easy guided reading books and the Story Retelling Rope or a few Comprehension Cards on display. At the Guided Writing Station, children should find a writing journal and pencil for each of them.

Explain to the children that they will be taking a book home to read every night. Emphasize that reading at home is vital to their success and that bringing the book back every day is their job. Send a letter to parents explaining the intervention and the importance of reading at home.

Station 1

Station 2

Station 3

Station 4

The First Day of RISE: Work on Procedures

Have students spend 12 to 15 minutes at each station on the first day. Because they will not have a familiar text to read at the Reread Yesterday's Book Station or to write about at the Guided Writing Station, have students read a short, easy book they can finish quickly. Then discuss that book with students at the Reread Yesterday's Book Station, and have them write about it at the Guided Writing Station.

 After you escort the children back to their classrooms, meet as a team to debrief the first session. What did you notice on day one? Share your thoughts with one another and prepare for tomorrow. This should only take a few minutes.

 TIP

On the first day of RISE, take a photo of each child and use the photos to create a poster titled "X-Grade Scholars." On the last day, add graduation caps to celebrate the group's accomplishment.

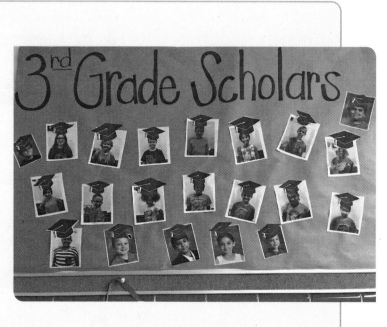

The Next Step Forward in Reading Intervention © 2018 by Jan Richardson and Ellen Lewis. Published by Scholastic Inc.

The Next Six to Eight Weeks

Implement the intervention over a six- to eight-week period for 45 to 60 minutes a day. As explained in Chapter 2, each station is led by an instructor and targets one of Jan's lesson components: read a new book, word study, reread and discuss the new book, and guided writing. Use anecdotal notes taken during the lesson and input from classroom teachers to plan lessons that target students' needs.

Remember, RISE is designed for students in grades 1 to 5, reading at text levels C–N, who need to improve decoding, spelling, fluency, writing, and retelling. For students who read above level N and only need to improve their comprehension, use the RISE Up procedures described in Chapters 5 and 6.

After the Intervention

After the RISE intervention, the team should prepare a comprehensive report for the classroom teacher, summarizing each child's reading, writing, and word study achievements. Include a final running record and Sight Word Chart. Recommend next steps for the classroom teacher. (See sample End-of-Program Report on page 65.)

 TIP

At the end of the intervention, schedule a time for RISE instructors to confer with classroom teachers to ensure the children continue to move forward when they return to classroom guided reading lessons.

MEETING IMPLEMENTATION CHALLENGES

Some schools have personnel and time constraints that can make implementing RISE a challenge. There are ways to make RISE work no matter what resources and time you have available.

45-Minute, Three-Station Model

If time is the issue, consider implementing a 45-minute, three-station model: Read a New Book, Phonics and Word Study, and Guided Writing. The activities from the Reread Yesterday's Book Station can be folded into Read a New Book. After reading the new book, the teacher leads students in a comprehension conversation.

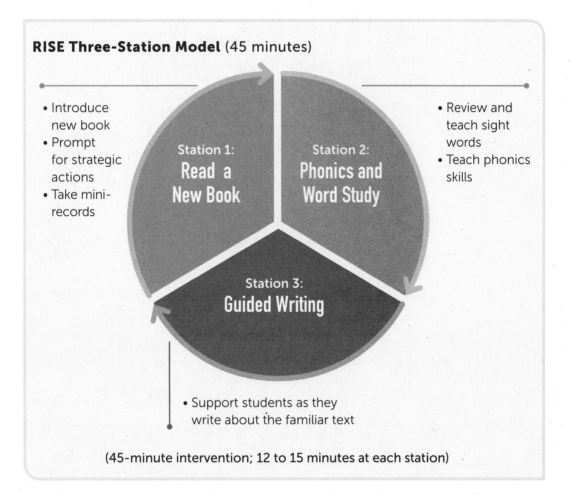

RISE Three-Station Model (45 minutes)

- Introduce new book
- Prompt for strategic actions
- Take mini-records

Station 1: Read a New Book

Station 2: Phonics and Word Study

- Review and teach sight words
- Teach phonics skills

Station 3: Guided Writing

- Support students as they write about the familiar text

(45-minute intervention; 12 to 15 minutes at each station)

60-Minute, Three-Station Model

If staffing is the primary challenge and you have only three instructors available to teach a 60-minute intervention, consider having students rotate to three stations: Read a New Book, Phonics and Word Study, and Guided Writing. During the last 12 to 15 minutes, they return to their first station to reread the book and have a comprehension conversation.

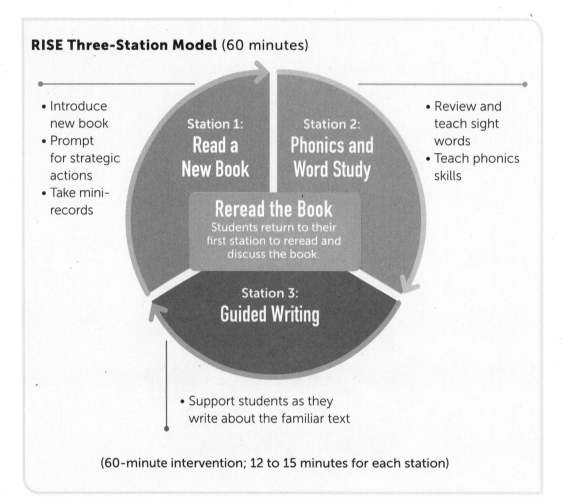

RISE Three-Station Model (60 minutes)

- Introduce new book
- Prompt for strategic actions
- Take mini-records

Station 1: Read a New Book

Station 2: Phonics and Word Study

Reread the Book
Students return to their first station to reread and discuss the book.

- Review and teach sight words
- Teach phonics skills

Station 3: Guided Writing

- Support students as they write about the familiar text

(60-minute intervention; 12 to 15 minutes for each station)

Single-Teacher, 40-Minute Model

Although the multi-instructor approach is a primary factor in RISE's success, we understand that some schools might not have the resources or support to involve so many people. If you teach striving readers at such a school, consider carrying out this single-teacher option, over six to eight weeks, with four students, using the instructional strategies and routines described in this chapter and Chapter 2:

- 15 minutes reading a new book
- 10 minutes of word study
- 15 minutes of guided writing

Be sure to give students a short movement break between activities to keep them energized and focused. It seems like a small thing, but it makes a big difference.

CHAPTER 4

What Is RISE Up?

RISE Up is a short-term comprehension intervention for children in grades 3 to 8 who read at text levels O–Z. Our research based on field-testing showed students who participated in six to eight weeks of RISE Up made 5.5 months of progress and showed significant improvement in comprehension, as measured on the *Next Step Guided Reading Assessment* (Richardson & Walther, 2013) and the *Benchmark Assessment System* (Fountas & Pinnell, 2016). For children reading at text levels C–N who need to improve skills in decoding, spelling, fluency, writing, and retelling, use the RISE procedures described in Chapters 2 and 3.

HOW DOES RISE UP WORK?

Three RISE Up instructors (e.g., special education teachers, Title I teachers, reading interventionists, ELL teachers, literacy coaches, retired teachers, student teachers, or teaching assistants) work with up to 12 students for 45 minutes a day over six to eight weeks. One of the instructors should be an expert in the reading process and able to train the other instructors in lesson procedures.

During the intensive 45-minute period, students are divided into three groups and rotate through three stations, where they read a short text (475 to 700 words) and respond to a comprehension strategy. During the two-day lesson, students read the same text three times but apply different comprehension strategies. This helps them develop flexible thinking and facilitates deeper comprehension. Or, students may read the same text two times and do guided writing, depending on what the instructors feel will benefit students most. The instructors remain at their station and repeat the lesson with each rotating group.

RISE Up: Reading Intervention for Students to Excel

For students in grades 3 to 8 who read at text levels O–Z

- Read new text (475 to 700 words)
- Teach literal comprehension strategy

Station 1:
Read a New Text for Literal Comprehension

Station 2:
Reread Yesterday's Text for Deeper Comprehension

- Reread the text
- Teach deeper comprehension strategy

Station 3:
Reread Yesterday's Text for Deeper Comprehension or Do Guided Writing

- Reread or write about the text

(45-minute intervention; 12 to 15 minutes at each station)

Strategies

Instructors must understand how to teach the 12 strategies described in Chapter 7 of *The Next Step Forward in Guided Reading* (Richardson, 2016).

1. Comprehension Monitoring
2. Retelling
3. Developing Vocabulary
4. Asking and Answering Questions
5. Identifying Main Idea and Details
6. Analyzing Characters
7. Analyzing Relationships

 TIP

When selecting short texts to use with students, consider complete magazine articles and books (not excerpts) between 475 and 700 words, fiction and nonfiction.

RISE UP

8. Inferring

9. Summarizing

10. Evaluating

11. Using Text Features

12. Understanding Text Structure

For training ideas, see the Professional Study Guide that accompanies the book at scholastic.com/NSFResources.

 The Next Step Forward in Reading Intervention © 2018 by Jan Richardson and Ellen Lewis. Published by Scholastic Inc.

Lesson Framework

Before meeting with the students, the three instructors choose a short text and two or three comprehension strategies. One of the strategies should target literal comprehension (Strategies 1–4) and be taught at Station 1. The others should target deeper comprehension (Strategies 5–12) and be taught at Stations 2 and 3 the following day. If you decide to do guided writing at Station 3, you will only need two comprehension strategies: a literal strategy for Station 1 and a deeper strategy for Station 2.

Literal Comprehension Strategies	Deeper Comprehension Strategies
1. Comprehension Monitoring	5. Identifying Main Idea and Details
2. Retelling	6. Analyzing Characters
3. Developing Vocabulary	7. Analyzing Relationships
4. Asking and Answering Questions	8. Inferring
	9. Summarizing
	10. Evaluating
	11. Using Text Features
	12. Understanding Text Structure

RISE UP

Although each station has a specific purpose, which is described on pages 93 to 98, all three instructors follow these general steps:

Step 1: Prepare students to read and think. Before students read the text, explain the comprehension strategy and tell them how to record their thinking. Depending on the focus, students might highlight text, circle key words, record inferences, create a graphic organizer, or write questions. Give them the appropriate Comprehension Card from Appendix R to guide their thinking and help them write short responses.

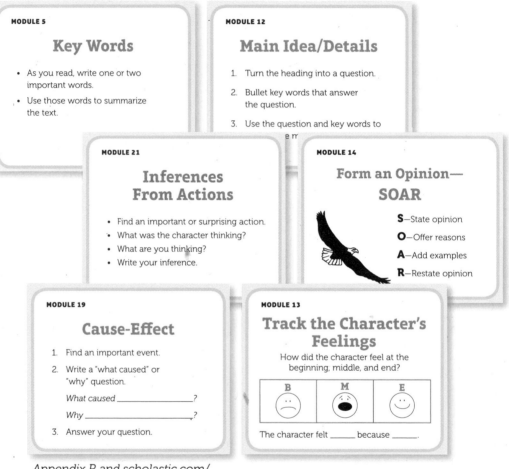

MODULE 5

Key Words

- As you read, write one or two important words.
- Use those words to summarize the text.

MODULE 12

Main Idea/Details

1. Turn the heading into a question.
2. Bullet key words that answer the question.
3. Use the question and key words to ~~e m~~

MODULE 21

Inferences From Actions

- Find an important or surprising action.
- What was the character thinking?
- What are you thinking?
- Write your inference.

MODULE 14

Form an Opinion— SOAR

S—State opinion

O—Offer reasons

A—Add examples

R—Restate opinion

MODULE 19

Cause-Effect

1. Find an important event.
2. Write a "what caused" or "why" question.

   What caused _____?

   Why _____?
3. Answer your question.

MODULE 13

Track the Character's Feelings

How did the character feel at the beginning, middle, and end?

B	M	E

The character felt _____ because _____.

Appendix R and scholastic.com/ NSFIntervention

Step 2: Read, write, and prompt. Have students read the text and take notes directly on it or in a separate journal. Their notes help them understand the text and help you assess their comprehension. As students read and write independently, work with individuals in a mini-reading conference, prompting them to share their thinking, pinpoint any confusing words or sentences, and explain their notes. Differentiate your prompting to meet the needs of the students. Below is a list of prompts for each comprehension strategy.

Prompts for Each Strategy

	Strategy	Prompts
1	Comprehension Monitoring	*Did that make sense? What part was confusing? What can you do to help yourself?*
2	Retelling	*What did you read? Who is the most important character, and what is he or she doing? Use your five fingers to retell the story.*
3	Developing Vocabulary	*Is there a word you don't understand? What can you do to figure it out? Can you substitute a word that makes sense? Explain the word to me.*
4	Asking and Answering Questions	*What are you wondering? What questions do you have? What are you thinking?*
5	Identifying Main Idea and Details	*What is the main idea of this paragraph (page)?* *What is the author saying about this topic? What are the most important details?*
6	Analyzing Characters	*What is the character feeling now? Why? What trait describes the character? What is your evidence? How has the character changed in the story?*

RISE UP

Prompts for Each Strategy

	Strategy	Prompts
7	**Analyzing Relationships**	*What caused...? What was the effect of...?* *What two ideas does the author compare? How are these ideas similar (or different)?*
8	**Inferring**	*What was a surprising action (or dialogue)? Why did the character do (or say) that? What is the character thinking?*
9	**Summarizing**	*What are three or four key words in the passage? Use those words and the main idea to summarize the passage.*
10	**Evaluating**	*What is the author's message? What are the different points of view in this passage? Why did the author write this piece? How is your opinion different from or similar to the author's? What lesson did the character learn? What is the theme?*
11	**Using Text Features**	*Explain this text feature. Why did the author include it? How does it help you understand the text?*
12	**Understanding Text Structure**	*What structure did the author use in this paragraph (or text)? Why do you think the author chose that structure?*

 The **Next Step Forward** in Reading Intervention © 2018 by Jan Richardson and Ellen Lewis. Published by Scholastic Inc.

Step 3: Discuss the text. During the final three to five minutes at each station, lead the group in a discussion in which students share their notes and challenge one another's thinking. You may want to prepare a few thought-provoking questions aimed at lifting students' processing levels. Encourage them to refer to their notes and the text as they contribute to the discussion. Below are some discussion starters for informational texts and narrative texts.

Text Type	Discussion Starters
Informational	• *What did you learn from this passage? What did you learn from the other passage we read on the same topic? How are the passages similar/different?* • *What is the main idea? What reasons and evidence did the author use to support the main idea?* • *What does the author want us to know or think?* • *Why did the author write this passage? What techniques did the author use to persuade us to agree with his or her opinion?* • *What is the author's point of view? What reasons did the author provide?* • *What is the structure of this text? Why do you think the author chose that structure?*
Narrative	• *What is the big idea/central message/lesson/moral? Why do you think that?* • *How is the theme of this text similar to or different from the theme of this other text we read?* • *What were the important events in this story? What was the climax?* • *Why is the setting important to the plot?* • *What traits describe the character(s)? What is your evidence?* • *What was the most important act the character did? What motivated the character to do that?* • *What can you infer about the character?* • *Describe the relationships between the characters. How do those relationships affect the plot?* • *Compare and contrast two characters or events. What is similar about them? What is different?*

Choosing Strategies and Modules

Use a comprehension assessment, such as *Next Step Guided Reading Assessment* (Richardson & Walther, 2013), anecdotal notes taken during lessons, and input from classroom teachers to select strategies. Always read your chosen text to ensure it's appropriate for teaching the strategies you picked.

1. Stop and Use Fix-Up Strategies
2. Stop, Think, Paraphrase (STP)
3. Beginning-Middle-End (B-M-E)
4. Five-Finger Retell
5. Key Words
6. Who-What
7. Strategies to Explain New Words
8. Green Questions
9. Red Questions
10. Very Important Part (V.I.P.) Fiction
11. Very Important Part (V.I.P.) Nonfiction
12. Turning Headings Into Questions
13. Track a Character's Feelings
14. Evidence of Character Traits
15. Who-What-Why
16. Action-Motivation Chart
17. Create a Sociogram
18. Compare and Contrast With Yellow Questions
19. Cause-Effect Questions
20. Inferences From Dialogue
21. Inferences From Actions
22. Inferences From a Character's Inner Thoughts
23. Drawing Conclusions
24. Somebody-Wanted-But-So (Then)
25. Key Word Summary
26. Thesis-Proof
27. Strategies to Enhance Comprehension
28. Graphic Organizers
29. Reciprocal Teaching

Each module lists progressive steps for a gradual release of responsibility. Begin with the first step of the module and move through the others as students gain proficiency. Each module has a Comprehension Card (Appendix R) that helps students think about the strategy and formulate a short response. The chart on the next two pages matches strategies to modules, and modules to Comprehension Cards.

The Top 12 Comprehension Strategies, Modules, and Cards

	Strategy	The reader...	Module	Comprehension Card
1	Comprehension Monitoring	is aware when meaning breaks down.	1	Fix-Up Strategies
2	Retelling	recalls information in nonfiction; retells story elements in fiction.	2 3 4 5 6	STP B-M-E, Shared Retelling (Appendix O) Five-Finger Retell Key Words Who-What
3	Developing Vocabulary	understands the meaning of a phrase or word.	7 29	Vocabulary Strategies Reciprocal Teaching
4	Asking and Answering Questions	asks and answers questions based on details in the text.	8 9 18 29	Green Questions Red Questions Yellow Questions Reciprocal Teaching
5	Identifying Main Idea and Details	is able to identify the main idea/central message and most important details.	10 11 12	V.I.P. Fiction V.I.P. Nonfiction Main Ideas/Details
6	Analyzing Characters (Fiction)	can identify character traits and motives.	13 14 15 16	Track the Character's Feelings Character—Trait—Evidence Form an Opinion—SOAR Who-What-Why Action-Motivation
7	Analyzing Relationships	expresses an understanding of relationships between people, events, or ideas.	17 18 19	Create a Sociogram Yellow Questions Cause-Effect

RISE UP

The Top 12 Comprehension Strategies, Modules, and Cards

	Strategy	The reader...	Module	Comprehension Card
8	Inferring	makes an inference or draws a conclusion from details in the text.	18 20 21 22 20–22 23	Who-What-Why Inferences From Dialogue Inferences From Actions Inferences From Inner Thoughts Make an Inference: Fiction Draw Conclusions
9	Summarizing	synthesizes information and prepares a condensed account that covers the main points.	24 25 29	SWBS Key Word Summary Reciprocal Teaching
10	Evaluating	understands the theme, author's purpose, point of view, and fact vs. opinion.	26	Thesis-Proof Form an Opinion—SOAR
11	Using Text Features	uses text features to clarify and extend understanding of the topic.	27	Text Features
12	Understanding Text Structure	understands how the author organizes the information within the text.	28	Text Structure Problem-Solution Compare & Contrast

 The Next Step Forward in Reading Intervention © 2018 by Jan Richardson and Ellen Lewis. Published by Scholastic Inc.

THE RISE UP STATIONS

Groups of four students rotate through three instructional stations:

- Station 1: Read a New Text for Literal Comprehension
- Station 2: Reread Yesterday's Text for Deeper Comprehension
- Station 3: Reread Yesterday's Text for Deeper Comprehension or Do Guided Writing

Station 1: Read a New Text for Literal Comprehension

For Station 1, the instructor focuses on reading for literal, or surface, understanding and clarifying unknown vocabulary by selecting one of the following:

- Comprehension Monitoring
- Retelling
- Developing Vocabulary
- Asking and Answering Questions

As stated earlier, each strategy is taught using a module that provides step-by-step guidelines for the instructor and a supporting Comprehension Card (Appendix R) for the students. For example, if the instructor chooses retelling (Strategy 2) as the focus, the students might do Stop, Think, Paraphrase (STP) (Module 2) or the Five-Finger Retell (Module 4). These modules teach for surface comprehension, which is a prerequisite to understanding text at a deeper level.

Give each student a copy of the text and provide a brief synopsis. Before reading, introduce new vocabulary that students aren't likely to figure out by using text clues. Have students highlight the words as you introduce them, using the following procedures.

1. **Define it.** Give a brief, kid-friendly definition. Do not ask students to define the word. It wastes time and causes confusion.

2. **Connect it.** Make a connection between the new word and students' background knowledge and experiences.

3. **Relate it to the text.** Tell students how the word is used in the text and direct them to a supportive illustration if one is provided.

4. **Turn and talk.** Ask students to explain the meaning of the word or give an example to the person sitting next to them.

Next, briefly explain the literal comprehension strategy students will be using, and distribute the Comprehension Card that matches the module. Have students read the text silently while you confer with them individually and take brief notes in the space provided on the back of the lesson plan. These notes will be used to help the other two instructors plan the next day's lesson. Close the lesson by leading a short discussion of the text.

By clarifying challenging vocabulary and firming up literal understanding, you prepare students to reread the text the following day with different comprehension strategies.

Signal the end of the station with a chime or bell. Tell students to put the text in their folders and move to their next station. The Station 1 instructor repeats the same lesson with each group; however, the prompting varies with each student.

> ▶ **VIDEO LINK**
>
> Station 1: Read a New Text
> for Literal Comprehension

Station 2: Reread Yesterday's Text for Deeper Comprehension

At Station 2, the four students reread the text used at Station 1 the previous day and apply a deeper comprehension strategy that the instructor chooses:

- Identifying Main Idea and Details
- Analyzing Characters
- Analyzing Relationships
- Inferring
- Summarizing
- Evaluating
- Using Text Features
- Understanding Text Structure

To teach the strategy, the instructor chooses a comprehension module—a different one from the module used at Station 1. Since the text is familiar, there is no need to introduce it. However, if it is the first time the students have practiced the module, they will need a short demonstration. Start by reading the Comprehension Card and modeling your thinking. Then have students read the text and write short responses that track their thinking. While students read and write independently, confer with them individually, reading their responses, asking clarifying questions, and prompting as needed. Record observations in the space provided on the back of the lesson plan. Lead a short discussion of the text during the last three to five minutes. Then have students move to their next station.

VIDEO LINK

Station 2: Reread Yesterday's Text for Deeper Comprehension

RISE UP

Station 3: Reread Yesterday's Text for Deeper Comprehension or Do Guided Writing

At this station, the four students read the same text they read at Station 2, but apply a different deeper comprehension strategy (Strategies 5–12), or they write for 12 to 15 minutes about the text.

TIP

If students need to improve decoding and spelling, include some of the word study activities described in Chapter 2.

Guided Writing Option

At Station 3, instructors have the option of doing a guided writing lesson instead of a second deeper comprehension strategy. That's because fluent readers need writing instruction just as much as instruction in comprehension. Give students writing prompts that frequently appear on your state's reading assessment, or choose from the Prompts for Guided Writing chart (page 98).

As students write, circulate among the group and assist individuals as necessary. After you read what students have written, teach something students can do to improve their writing. One student might need to reread what he or she has written to check for accuracy. Another may need guidance on how to increase sentence variation. A third may be ready to combine sentences using conjunctions or introductory clauses. Regardless of your teaching points, always remember that the goal of each interaction is not to "fix" the writing, but to teach something that will make the student a better writer.

> ☀ **TIP**
>
> *If students need help getting started, dictate the first sentence of the response. Then scaffold them as they construct the rest of their sentences.*

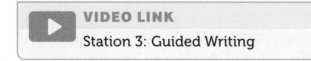

▶ **VIDEO LINK**
Station 3: Guided Writing

RISE UP

Prompts for Guided Writing

Narrative
- What traits describe the character? Use examples from the story to support your opinion.
- Summarize the major events. Why are those events important?
- Contrast two characters and their points of view.
- Write about the theme. What lesson(s) did the character learn? What lesson(s) can you learn from this story?
- Select an important action the character did. What motivated the character to do that?
- At first, how does ____ feel about ____? How does he/she feel about it later? Use details from the story in your answer.
- Identify a character trait to describe ____. How does this trait help the character (or another character)? Use details from the text to support your answer.
- Describe how ____'s feelings change throughout the story. Use details from the text to support your answer.
- How do you think ____ felt after ____? Use details from the text to support your answer.

Informational
- Write a summary of the topic using the two texts we read. Include examples from both texts.
- Describe the author's point of view and support it with evidence from the text.
- Describe your point of view (opinion) and support it with evidence from the text.
- Explain how the author uses evidence to support particular points in the text.
- Compare and contrast two ideas.
- Describe two or more effects of ____. Use details from the book in your answer.
- Describe the causes and effects of ____.
- Write a summary of the text. Include the main idea and three or more details.
- What two facts (ideas, concepts) found in the text do you think are the most important in the passage? Why do you think so? Use specific details from the text to support your answer.

  The Next Step Forward in Reading Intervention © 2018 by Jan Richardson and Ellen Lewis. Published by Scholastic Inc.

RISE Up Intervention Lesson Plan

Station 1: Read a New Text for Literal Comprehension

Text Title:	Date:	Comprehension Focus (Strategies 1–4 listed on page 85):
The Smuggler	12/10	Retelling (2)

Synopsis of the Text:

A clever smuggler tricks an inspector for many years.
How does he do it?

New Vocabulary:

burdened, exasperated

Read With Prompting
Using Module
2 – STP   Stop, Think, Paraphrase

Station 2: Reread Yesterday's Text for Deeper Comprehension

Text Title:	Date:	Comprehension Focus (Strategies 5–12 listed on page 85):
Kids Need More ZZZs	12/10	Analyzing Relationships

Read With Prompting
Using Module
19 – Cause-Effect Questions

cause	effect
caffeine TV	lack of focus accident prone

Station 3: Reread Yesterday's Text for Deeper Comprehension or **Do Guided Writing**

Text Title:	Date:	Comprehension Focus (Strategies 5–12 listed on page 85):
Kids Need More ZZZs	12/10	Analyzing Relationships (7)

Read With Prompting
Using Module
19 – Cause-Effect Questions

Guided Writing Prompt:

What causes children not to get enough sleep? (TV, caffeine)
What are the effects? (Less focus, safety, health)

The Next Step Forward in Reading Intervention © 2018 by Jan Richardson and Ellen Lewis, Scholastic Inc. • scholastic.com   139

Appendix E and scholastic.com/NSFIntervention

RISE Up Intervention Lesson Plan

Observations: Record each student's understanding of the strategy, using ths rubric.
(1) Not Independent (2) Somewhat Independent (3) Almost Independent (4) Independent

Name: Simona (2) Prompted for the cause.	Name: Daniel (2) Confused by the chart.
Name: Amy (2) Prompted to reread the passage to find the cause. Knew the effect.	Name: Ashin (4) Quickly understood cause-effect. Completed chart w/o support. Added inferences.
Name: John (2) Prompted to explain the difference between cause & effect (reason — what happens).	Name: Christopher (4) Completed chart w/o support. Explained purpose of the bar graph.
Name: Melanie (1) Needs support with vocabulary. Confused about the text.	Name: Maya (3) Good cause-effect chart. Needed some support.
Name: Allison (3) Understood cause-effect. Needed support understanding bar graph.	Name: Keidy (2) Prompted for the cause. What is the <u>reason</u> kids don't get enough sleep?
Name: Teyo (4) Great cause-effect chart. Explained the purpose of the text feature.	Name: Antonio (3) Showed improvement in understanding cause-effect relationships.

Next Steps

Use cause-effect strategy with a different text. Share chart with classroom teachers and help them plan a mini-lesson on cause-effect.

Appendix E and scholastic.com/NSFIntervention

Using RISE Up: An Example

This section shows how students can use *The Smuggler*, a short folk tale with a twist, to practice three different comprehension strategies. On Day 1 at Station 1, the students read *The Smuggler* for the first time, using Module 7, to develop vocabulary. On Day 2 at Stations 2 and 3, they reread the tale for deeper comprehension. Specifically, at Station 2 they use Module 23 to learn how to draw conclusions, and at Station 3 they use Module 16 to flag important actions and analyze a character's motivation.

The Smuggler

A Folktale From the Middle East

A clever smuggler led a donkey burdened with bundles of straw to the border between two lands. The inspector at the border eyed the donkey's bundles with suspicion.

"You must allow me to search your bundles!" the inspector said. "I think that you have hidden a valuable treasure that you wish to sell at the market. If so, you must pay me a border fee!"

"Search as you wish," said the man. "If you find something other than straw, I will pay whatever fee you ask."

The inspector pulled apart the straw bundles until there was straw in the air, straw on the ground, straw, straw all around. Yet not a valuable thing in the straw was found.

"You are a clever smuggler!" said the inspector. "I am certain that you are hiding something. Yet so carefully have you covered it, I have not discovered it. Go!"

The man crossed the border with his donkey. The suspicious inspector looked on with a scowl.

The next day, the man came back to the border with a donkey burdened with straw. Once again the inspector pulled apart the bundles. There was straw in the air, straw on the ground, straw, straw, straw all around. "Not one valuable thing have I found!" the exasperated inspector said. "Go!"

The man and the donkey went across the border. "Bah!" cried the inspector once again, scowling.

The next day and the next day, for ten years, the man came to the border with a donkey burdened with straw. Each day the inspector searched his bundles, but he found nothing.

Finally, the inspector retired. Even as an old man, he could not stop thinking about that clever smuggler. One day as he walked through the marketplace, still trying to solve the mystery at the border, he muttered, "I am certain that man was smuggling something. Perhaps I should have looked more carefully in the donkey's mouth. Or he could have hidden something between the hairs on the donkey's tail!"

As he mumbled to himself, he noticed a familiar face in the crowd. "You!" he exclaimed. "I know you! You were the man who came to the border every day with a donkey burdened with straw. Come and speak with me!"

When the man walked toward him, the old inspector said, "Admit it! You were smuggling something across the border, weren't you?" The man nodded and grinned.

"Aha!" said the old inspector. "Just as I suspected. You were sneaking something to market! Tell me what it was! What were you smuggling? Tell me, if you can."

"Donkeys," said the man.

"The Smuggler" from *Wisdom Tales From Around the World* by Heather Forest (August House, 1996).

148   SCHOLASTIC TEACHING RESOURCES   *Guided Reading in Grades 3–6*

Continued on next page

Using RISE Up: An Example
Continued

DAY 1
Focus: Strategies to Explain New Words
(Module 7, Progressive Step 4)

- Instructor covers the words *burdened*, *inspector*, *retired*, and *scowling*.
- Students write a synonym that would make sense in the sentence.

DAY 2
Focus: Inferring by Drawing Conclusions
(Module 23, Progressive Step 3)

- Instructor uses a sticky note to cover the last sentence.
- Students complete the chart:

I read...	I know...	I conclude...

Station 1: Read a New Text for Literal Comprehension

Station 2: Reread Yesterday's Text for Deeper Comprehension

Station 3: Reread Yesterday's Text for Deeper Comprehension or Do Guided Writing

DAY 2
Focus: Analyzing Characters, Action-Motivation Chart
(Module 16, Progressive Step 2)

- Students complete the chart:

Character	Action	Motivation

Practice Reading

Encourage RISE Up students to select interesting books to practice reading in school and at home. It's not a problem if the books are below their instructional level. Reading "easy" books builds fluency and comprehension (Allington, 2009).

TEAM MEETINGS AND LESSON PLANNING

After students return to class, the three instructors meet for about five minutes to share their observations and concerns. This helps them plan the next day's lessons. For example, perhaps the Station 1 instructor used the STP (Stop, Think, Paraphrase) module and noticed students did well paraphrasing each paragraph but needed more work on retelling the entire passage. The next day the students could work on summarizing the text at Station 2, using Module 24, Somebody-Wanted-But-So (Then). If the Station 3 instructor notices that students are having difficulty making inferences, he or she may choose Module 15, Who-What-Why, or Module 23, Drawing Conclusions, to strengthen students' use of the strategy. The daily opportunity for the team to reflect on the lesson and make decisions about the next lesson is one of the many strengths of RISE Up. It helps teachers monitor progress, celebrate successes, analyze concerns, and plan a clear path for taking students to the next step in their literacy journey.

▶ **VIDEO LINK**
RISE Up Team Meeting

Monitoring Progress

Although assessing progress in comprehension can be challenging, there are several ways to do it. One way is to use a simple rubric to measure proficiency on a strategy.

1. Not independent (needs extensive support)

2. Somewhat independent (needs some support)

3. Almost independent (needs very little support)

4. Independent (requires no support)

On the lesson plan, record the number, 1 to 4, that correlates to the level of support you provided each student.

Another option is to assess how students employ the strategy when reading self-selected books on their own. Every two weeks, take the final three to five minutes at each station to ask students about their independent reading. Have students talk about their book, using the comprehension strategy they just practiced at the station.

Still another option is to do a Comprehension Interview with each student at another time of the day so it doesn't take time from the intervention lessons.

See pages 221 to 226.

Connecting With Classroom Teachers

Whenever possible, have the entire RISE Up team attend grade-level meetings. Share your insights about individual students. At the end of the eight-week intervention, administer a formal assessment to students, such as *Next Step Guided Reading Assessment* (Richardson & Walther, 2013), *Developmental Reading Assessment* (Beaver, 2012), or *Benchmark Assessment System* (Fountas & Pinnell, 2016). Write a summary of progress on each student for the classroom teacher, and suggest strategies to emphasize in guided reading lessons. (See sample on the next page.)

RISE Up will enrich students' literacy experiences and create ripples of success in whole-class work, during independent reading time, and in every subject area. The next chapter will guide you in creating a smooth and successful implementation.

RISE Up: End-of-Program Report

Student	Entry Level	Exit Level	# of Lessons	Notes for Classroom Teachers
Jeffrey	N	Q	36	**COMPREHENSION SKILLS:** Strong decoder. Literal strategies in place. Now applying some deeper strategies. Strong gains in inferring. Uses text features to clarify understanding a topic. Looks for evidence in the text, no more guessing or inventing responses. **WRITING:** Large bank of known sight words. Beginning to use more complex sentence structures as comprehension skills deepen. **RECOMMENDATIONS:** Continue to practice identifying main idea and details.
Steven	N	P	39	**COMPREHENSION SKILLS:** Literal strategies in place. Can now analyze characters and relationships. Shows strength in deepening comprehension with cause-effect and compare & contrast. **WRITING:** Likes to insert charts in nonfiction. Strong at summarizing using SWBS(T). **RECOMMENDATIONS:** Work on inferring and drawing conclusions. Give him extra processing time on Make an Inference: Fiction.
Tianna	M	O	38	**COMPREHENSION SKILLS:** Literal strategies in place. Decoding and comprehension skills have improved. Showed the most gains in analyzing characters, analyzing relationships, and inferring. **WRITING:** Large bank of known sight words. Writes several sentences, some complex. **RECOMMENDATIONS:** Focus on summarizing, using Key Word Summary for practice.
Justin	N	Q	38	**COMPREHENSION SKILLS:** Good decoder. Literal strategies in place. Prefers nonfiction, and most gains in Make an Inference: Nonfiction. Strong gains in summarizing using Key Word Summary. **WRITING:** Uses text features to write coherent, logical nonfiction summaries. **RECOMMENDATIONS:** Provide practice in retelling fiction using STP, Who-What, and SWBS(T).
Marianna	O	Q	40	**COMPREHENSION SKILLS:** Good decoder. Strong gains in identifying main idea and details in fiction and nonfiction. Includes supporting details in retellings without prompting. **WRITING:** Loves to write, but needs to be careful to reread her work to check for omitted words. **RECOMMENDATIONS:** Work on analyzing relationships. Use Cause-Effect lessons because she tends to mix up the cause and the effect while reading.
Chris	N	P	40	**COMPREHENSION SKILLS:** Exhibited early inferring skills, but did not pay attention to detail when Green and Red Questions were used. With prompting, he has started slowing down to include the literal in his strong inferring and is aware of how this affects his answers. He is pausing to check literal answers and to more accurately summarize using Key Word Summary. **WRITING:** Strong gains in composing sentences that make sense, but he needs to say each word as he writes to improve accuracy. **RECOMMENDATIONS:** He can think deeply about his reading but needs to practice slowing down and paying attention to literal details. He uses Comprehension Cards as prompts to check and complete his thinking, and should continue to do so.

RISE UP

CHAPTER 5

RISE Up in Action

As with the RISE program, RISE Up calls for partnering with a team of stakeholders. So, the first step in implementing the intervention is to meet with the principal, classroom teachers, reading teachers, specialists, and intervention teachers to explain the program. RISE Up is an intensive, short-term intervention for up to 12 students at a time in grades 3 to 8 who can fluently decode and retell text at levels O–Z, but struggle to comprehend at a deeper level. Utilizing the comprehension strategies found in Chapter 7 of *The Next Step Forward in Guided Reading* (Richardson, 2016), RISE Up creates flexible thinkers who learn to respond to text in a variety of ways. After only six to eight weeks of instruction, students demonstrate confidence and improved comprehension skills that ensure success across all subjects. You can use the PowerPoint and videos provided on the resource website (scholastic.com/NSFIntervention) during this orientation meeting.

PREPARING FOR RISE UP

As you implement this intervention, be sure to address all the topics described in this section.

Schedule a Time

Ask the administrators and classroom teachers to allocate 45 minutes every day for RISE Up. If possible, schedule it during the language arts block or designated intervention time so students do not miss content area instruction. Some schools use their extended day, special intervention period, or after-school program.

Locate a Space

Find a room large enough to accommodate up to 12 students, three instructors, and three stations. If space is limited, consider using the cafeteria or any other available room.

Station 1: Read a New Text for Literal Comprehension

Station 2: Reread Yesterday's Text for Deeper Comprehension

Station 3: Reread Yesterday's Text for Deeper Comprehension or Do Guided Writing

Train the Instructors

The RISE Up leader should be an experienced reading teacher who can train the other members of the team, monitor student progress, and assist with lesson planning.

Each instructor needs to learn how to teach a fluent guided reading lesson and the 29 comprehension modules described in *The Next Step Forward in Guided Reading*. Model and practice the procedures described in Chapters 6 and 7, and watch the accompanying video clips. You may want to invite classroom teachers to join the group. Video clips and the *Professional Study Guide* are available at scholastic.com/NSFResources.

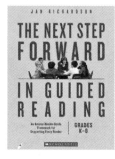

See Chapters 6 and 7.

Gather Materials

Because students will be reading a new text every day at Station 1, you will need about 40 short articles or stories, from 475 to 700 words, that are close to the group's instructional reading level. We use short texts because students can read them in a 15-minute session, and they resemble the kinds of texts students are expected to read for most state tests. Here are some resources for short texts:

- Scholastic Short Reads (teacher.scholastic.com/products/guidedreading/shortreads.htm)
- Scholastic magazines (classroommagazines.scholastic.com)
- Scholastic Teaching Resources books with reproducible passages
- ReadWorks.org
- Newsela.com
- The Comprehension Toolkit (heinemann.com/comprehensiontoolkit)

Each student needs a two-pocket folder for storing articles and stories. You will need the following instructional materials for each station.

Instructional Materials for Each Station		
Station 1: Read a New Text	**Station 2: Reread Yesterday's Text**	**Station 3: Reread Yesterday's Text or Do Guided Writing**
• Multiple copies of a new short text (1 per student) • Sticky notes and flags • Highlighters and pencils • 4 copies of each Comprehension Card from Modules 1–8 (Appendix R and scholastic.com/NSFIntervention) • Notebook or journal	• Multiple copies of yesterday's Station 1 short text • Sticky notes and flags • Highlighters and pencils • 4 Character Feelings and Traits Charts (Appendix Q and scholastic.com/NSFIntervention) • 4 copies of each Comprehension Card from Modules 9–29 (Appendix R and scholastic.com/NSFIntervention) • Notebook or journal	• Multiple copies of yesterday's Station 1 short text • Sticky notes and flags • Highlighters and pencils • 4 Character Feelings and Traits Charts (Appendix Q and scholastic.com/NSFIntervention) • 4 copies of each Comprehension Card from Modules 9–29 (Appendix R and scholastic.com/NSFIntervention) • Guided Writing Page Template (Appendix P and scholastic.com/NSFIntervention) • 4 Personal Word Walls (Appendix S and scholastic.com/NSFIntervention)

 TIP

Put copies of the text in plastic sleeves so students can use dry-erase markers to record their notes. That way, you can reuse articles and stories.

Assess the Students

You will need a reading assessment that specifically identifies students who can decode well but struggle with comprehension. We recommend *Next Step Guided Reading Assessment* (Richardson & Walther, 2013), a classroom-tested assessment kit that provides a complete picture of each reader's word knowledge, phonics skills, fluency, and comprehension. Two of the four assessments (Whole-Class Comprehension Assessment and the Individual Reading Conference) target specific comprehension strategies, which can be used to select strategies to teach in the RISE Up lessons.

Select a RISE Up Group

For each grade, create a chart that lists student names and assessment data. Use the list and classroom observations to determine which students should be selected for the first round of the RISE Up intervention.

Then subdivide them into three groups so they can rotate through the stations. To allow for personalized and targeted instruction, keep the subgroups small, no more than four students.

Throughout the intervention, watch for students who lag behind the group, and intervene before they become frustrated. Students making significantly slower progress should exit RISE Up and enter an alternative intervention. They can reenter RISE Up with another group of students later in the year. Keep a waiting list of potential RISE Up candidates.

Remember, RISE Up is designed for third through eighth graders who fluently read at text levels O–Z but need to improve comprehension. For students who read below level O and need to improve decoding, fluency, and retelling, use RISE.

RISE Up: 4th Grade, March

Student	Instructional Reading Level	Teacher	Group #
Gabriel	O	Hanson	3
Teyo	N	Hanson	1
Ashir	N	Hanson	1
Melanie	P	Hanson	3
John	P	Hanson	3
Amy	P	Hanson	2
Resham	N	Lounsbury	1
Simona	P	Lounsbury	2
Daniel	O	Lounsbury	2
Allisson	O	Lounsbury	1
Erick	O	Lounsbury	2
Keidy	P	Lounsbury	3

RISE Up student roster

IMPLEMENTING RISE UP

Before you begin instruction, meet with students to explain the intervention, introduce the materials, and teach routines and procedures.

Orientation Day

Bring students to the RISE Up room for about 20 minutes of orientation. Explain that they have been chosen for RISE Up so they can become better readers. Divide them into three groups and send each group to one of the stations. Have an engaging text and Comprehension Cards at each station. Include writing journals at Station 3 if you choose the guided writing option instead of a second deeper comprehension strategy. The instructor at each station will briefly explain the procedures and have the students practice using the materials. After a few minutes, ring a chime or bell and have students move to the next station. Repeat the rotations until students have visited each station and practiced the routines.

 TIP

Teach students routines and procedures for RISE Up. Explain what happens at each station and how to rotate. This ensures efficient use of time.

RISE UP

Station 1

Station 2

Station 3

The First Day of RISE Up: Work on Procedures

Have students spend 12 to 15 minutes at each station on the first day. Because they will not have a familiar text to read in Stations 2 and 3, use the same short text several levels below their instructional level. Then have them practice a different comprehension strategy at each station.

The Next Six to Eight Weeks

Implement the intervention over a six- to eight-week period for 45 minutes every day following the procedures in Chapter 4. Students rotate to three stations each day: reading a new text, rereading yesterday's text, and rereading yesterday's text again or writing about it.

After the Intervention

After the RISE Up intervention, the team should prepare a comprehensive report for the classroom teacher summarizing each child's reading achievements. Include a final running record, and recommend next steps for the classroom teacher. (See sample End-of-Program Report on page 105.)

TIP

Have students walk to RISE Up independently, as opposed to a teacher escorting them, to eliminate the stigma often associated with traditional pull-out programs.

TIP

At the end of the intervention, schedule a time for RISE Up instructors to confer with classroom teachers to ensure students continue to move forward when they return to classroom guided reading lessons.

ADAPTING RISE UP FOR THE CLASSROOM

RISE Up can be adapted for classroom guided reading instruction. Over two days, students read a new text for literal comprehension, write about the text independently, and reread the text for deeper comprehension. (See sample lesson plan on pages 117 to 118.)

Select the Text

Use assessment results to group students according to their comprehension needs, and select a short, slightly challenging text for each group. Do not use the same text for every group. Students should be able to decode the text with little teacher support; their challenge should come from applying the comprehension strategy. Use a variety of genres and, when possible, choose topics that align to what they're being taught in social studies and/or science.

Read a New Text *(15 minutes)*

On Day 1, students read a new text for literal, or surface, comprehension. For the comprehension focus, consult pages 90 and 91 to select one of the first four strategies and then a module and Comprehension Card that supports it. After a brief introduction, students read the text independently and write short responses, applying the comprehension strategy. The teacher confers with individual students, asking questions, clarifying confusions, and prompting for comprehension. During the last three minutes, students share their notes and discuss the text. Before students leave the station, the teacher explains the independent writing assignment.

For detailed instructions on how to teach each module, see Chapter 7.

Independent Writing *(15 minutes)*

On Day 1 or Day 2, students independently write a response to the text. Ideally, this writing is done on the same day as the reading, but if the group meets at the end of the guided reading block, students should write their responses the following day.

Before writing, students should always draft a simple plan or concept map, using key words and phrases from the text. Students who struggle with writing should also receive guided writing instruction during other guided reading lessons. Suggested writing prompts are listed on page 98.

Reread the Text for Deeper Comprehension *(15 minutes)*

On Day 2, students meet with the teacher and reread the text from the previous day, using a different comprehension strategy. Use Modules 9–29 listed on page 90 for teaching ideas to support deeper thinking. Students should also bring the responses they wrote at the Independent Writing Station. Because students are familiar with the text, no introduction is needed. While students reread, the teacher confers with individuals and probes for deeper comprehension. Students spend the last few minutes discussing the text and sharing their written responses with the group.

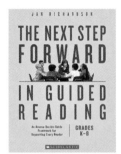

For detailed instructions on how to teach each module, see Chapter 7.

Adapting RISE Up
for Classroom Guided Reading: An Example

Here is an example of how to adapt the RISE Up framework for guided reading. Before meeting with the group, the teacher chose a short, informational text called "The Talkative Turtle." On Day 1, she taught students to ask and answer questions, using Module 8, Green Questions. Then the students wrote responses to the text independently, using the Character Feelings and Traits Charts in Appendix Q and at scholastic.com/NSFIntervention.

On Day 2, the teacher taught inferring using Module 20, Inferences From Dialogue. Then students discussed the text, using their notes and independent writing.

The Talkative Turtle

A Wisdom Tale From Ancient India

Long ago in India, there lived a turtle who was always talking. His endless chatter annoyed the creatures who shared the pond, and they avoided him. He spent his days mumbling to himself as he climbed in and out of the water.

One day, two visiting geese landed along the shore. The turtle admired their sleek feathers, and spent many hours praising their beauty. At last, to avoid the turtle's ceaseless chatter, the geese prepared to fly off to another pond. "Take me with you!" cried the turtle. "I am lonely here, and you are fine company."

"How can we do such a thing?" asked the birds. "You cannot fly."

"Nothing is impossible," said the turtle. "I will think of a plan."

To the amusement of the geese, the turtle said, "It is quite simple. First, let us find a long, strong stick. Each of you can hold one end of it in your beak. I will then bite hard in the middle. When you fly up together, I will cling to the center of the stick with my strong mouth. That way you can carry me over the trees."

The geese replied, "What a ridiculous idea! You could fall to your death!"

The turtle protested, "I will not fall. My mouth is strong. I will hold on tightly."

"Your mouth is strong from endless talking," squawked the geese "You will be safe only if you can keep your mouth shut."

Indignantly, the turtle replied, "You think that I cannot keep quiet, but I can. I know when to be silent and when to speak. Admit it. My idea is excellent. Let me try my invention and fly with you."

"Very well," said the geese. "But we cannot guarantee your safety on this journey."

"Then go and get the stick," ordered the turtle. "You'll see how quiet I can be when silence is important."

The geese flew off and returned with a long, strong stick. They both took an end in their beaks. The turtle clamped his mouth onto the middle. As the geese beat their wings and flew into the air, the dangling turtle went up too.

Soaring high above the trees, they were a vision to behold. Some children at play looked up and noticed the strange trio. "Look! Look!" cried one child. "Two geese are carrying a turtle on a stick!"

Another child chimed in, "What clever birds! They thought of a way to carry turtles!"

Another cheered, "Good thinking, geese!"

The turtle heard the children's voices. Their words infuriated him. He fumed, "They should be complimenting me for this fine plan, not the geese." Outraged, the turtle exploded with sound.

"It was my idea!" he sputtered, as he tumbled to the ground.

Reprinted from the November/December 1998 edition of Storyworks magazine.

Guided Reading in Grades 3–6 SCHOLASTIC TEACHING RESOURCES 149

Continued on next page

RISE UP

Adapting the RISE Up Framework for Guided Reading: An Example

Continued

The Talkative Turtle

A Wisdom Tale From Ancient India

DAY 1
Read a New Text

Strategy: Asking and Answering Questions
(Module 8: Green Questions)

Assign independent writing response.

DAY 1 or 2
Independent Writing

Compare and contrast characters using the Character Feelings and Traits Charts.

DAY 3
Reread the Text

Strategy: Inferring
(Module 20: Inferences From Dialogue)

Students bring independent writing response to guided reading to use during discussion.

Whether you implement RISE Up as an intervention program or as part of classroom guided reading instruction, students will become flexible thinkers, equipped with deeper comprehension skills and newfound confidence. Expect students to apply strategies they learn whenever they engage in independent reading.

RISE Up Classroom Lesson Plan

Text Title:	Dates:
The Talkative Turtle	1/24-1/25

Day 1: Read a New Text for Literal Comprehension

Comprehension Focus (Strategies 1–4 listed on page 85): Asking and Answering Questions (4)	Module # __8__ Green Questions

Synopsis of the Text:
Long ago, there was a turtle who would not stop talking.
He had an idea but it would only work if he kept quiet. Could he?

New Vocabulary:

mumbling, ceaseless, indignantly

Read With Prompting. Discussion Prompt:
What did the geese think of the turtle's idea? Why?
Students ask and answer each other's questions.

Day 1 or 2: Independent Writing

Writing Prompt:
Compare and contrast the characters using the Character Feelings and Traits Chart.

Day 2: Reread the Text for Deeper Comprehension

Comprehension Focus (Strategies 5–12 listed on page 85): Inferring (8)	Module # 20 Inferences From Dialogue

Read With Prompting: Discussion Prompt:
Students bring independent writing response to guided reading to use during discussion.

Appendix F and scholastic.com/NSFIntervention

RISE UP

RISE Up Classroom Lesson Plan

Observations: Record each student's understanding of the strategy, using this rubric.
(1) Not Independent (2) Somewhat Independent (3) Almost Independent (4) Independent

Name: Anthony Vocabulary strategies (3) Discussion Prompt (3) Inferring from dialogue (3)	Name: Tanwa Vocabulary strategies (1) Discussion Prompt (2) Inferring from dialogue (2)
Name: Sharif Vocabulary strategies (2) Discussion Prompt (3) Inferring from dialogue (2)	Name: Julie Vocabulary strategies (3) Discussion Prompt (3) Inferring from dialogue (4)
Name: Amanda Vocabulary strategies (4) Discussion Prompt (4) Inferring from dialogue (3)	Name: Jose Vocabulary strategies (3) Discussion Prompt (3) Inferring from dialogue (2)

Next Steps
- Continue using Module 7, Strategies to Explain New Words, with fiction texts. Select texts that include text clues for determining unfamiliar words.
- Use the Character Feelings and Traits Chart during discussion and writing.
- Repeat Module 20, Step 2, Inferences From Dialogue, on the next lesson.
- Julie is ready for Module 21, Inferences From Actions.
- Jose is ready for Step 3 of Module 20. Have him flag the dialogue where he makes an inference.

Appendix F and scholastic.com/NSFIntervention

Single-Teacher, 40-Minute Model

If you don't have the resources and support to implement the multi-instructor RISE Up model, consider this single-teacher option:

- Students read a new text for literal comprehension. Use Strategies 1–4 and Modules 1–8 listed on pages 90–92 for instruction. (15 minutes)

- Students reread the same text for deeper comprehension. Use Strategies 5–12 and Modules 9–29 listed on pages 90–92 for instruction. (10 minutes)

- Students write about the text with teacher support and guidance. (15 minutes)

Work with four students, over six to eight weeks, using the instructional strategies and routines described in this chapter and Chapter 4. To keep the energy level high, remember to give the students a short movement break between activities.

RISE UP

CHAPTER 6

Family Engagement: RISE With Literacy

Parental involvement is important for the educational success of all children, not just for those who struggle with literacy. RISE With Literacy, an after-school event for all K–2 families, is a terrific way to strengthen strategies taught in the classroom and during the RISE intervention. Showing parents how to do strategies with their children builds a literacy partnership between home and school.

"RISE WITH LITERACY" NIGHTS

At the event, families rotate through three stations.

Station 1: Introduction *(10 minutes)*

Parents and children meet in any large space for a brief welcome and presentation that explains the stations and encourages parents to read with their children at home. Consider using the downloadable PowerPoint presentation at scholastic.com/NSFIntervention.

Station 2: Demonstration and Practice *(30 minutes)*

Parents and children go to a kindergarten, first-grade, or second-grade classroom to learn a comprehension strategy from *The Next Step Forward in Guided Reading*. In each classroom, the station leader gathers students and spends about 15 minutes reading a picture book and modeling the strategy. Then, children join their parents at a table to read books and practice the strategy the leader modeled. The accompanying Comprehension Cards (Appendix R) are placed on the table for parents to use and take home.

Station 3: Take-Home Book *(10 minutes)*

Before leaving for home, everyone moves to Station 3 for refreshments. Each student chooses a free book to take home.

FAMILY ENGAGEMENT

Preparing for the Event

At the beginning of the school year, establish dates for two or three "RISE With Literacy" nights and enter them in the school calendar.

Step 1: Recruit Classroom Teachers

During a staff meeting, introduce RISE With Literacy. Ask teachers to volunteer as greeters, helpers, or station leaders. Because there are three separate Station 2s (kindergarten, first grade, and second grade), recruit at least three leaders who are comfortable teaching the strategies. (You don't want more than 35 children and parents at a Station 2, so plan accordingly if you are at a large school.)

Step 2: Gather Giveaway Books

Ask libraries, bookstores, and parents to donate books to hand out at Station 3. You can also apply for a grant or ask local organizations and businesses to donate money to purchase new or gently used books. Seeking donations early will ensure every student receives a book to take home.

Step 3: Choose Strategies and Procedures

Several weeks before the event, ask each Station 2 leader to select one comprehension strategy and a procedure (described in Chapter 7 of *The Next Step Forward in Guided Reading*) for teaching it—ideally, a strategy and procedure taught during whole-class lessons and guided reading. Because they're the easiest for parents to do with young children, comprehension monitoring, retelling, asking and answering questions, analyzing characters, and inferring are good choices for strategies, using the following procedures.

Appendix R and scholastic.com/NSFIntervention

Step 4: Gather Materials

Each Station 2 leader will need:

- a picture book to read to students to model the strategy. Big Books work best. You can turn any picture book into a Big Book by using an interactive whiteboard or a document camera to display each page onto a blank wall.

- 40 to 50 guided reading books for parents to use with their children.

- copies of the Comprehension Card to give to parents.

Step 5: Communicate With Parents

The following ideas will ensure good attendance:

- Introduce RISE With Literacy at back-to-school night.

- In the school newsletter, advertise upcoming "RISE With Literacy" nights.

- Create a RISE With Literacy banner for your school's website, with a link to a description.

- Have participating teachers visit K–2 classrooms and explain the event to children.

- One week before the event, give each K–2 student a RISE With Literacy RSVP letter to take home (Appendix U).

- On the night before the event, send a prerecorded phone message to every K–2 parent (Appendix V).

- On the day of the event, send every child home wearing a "Take me to RISE With Literacy tonight at _____ P.M." sticker.

Countdown to RISE With Literacy

When	What to Do
Beginning of the year	• Choose dates and introduce RISE With Literacy to the staff. • Ask kindergarten, first-, and second-grade teachers to volunteer. • Inform parents of upcoming "RISE With Literacy" nights. • Start gathering books to give away at the event.
Two weeks before the event	• Plan Station 2 with K–2 teachers. Choose three strategies (one per grade level) and procedures from Chapter 7 in *The Next Step Forward in Guided Reading*. • Gather teaching materials: read-aloud books, guided reading books, and copies of Comprehension Cards.
One week before the event	• Send home the RISE With Literacy RSVP Letter to Parents (Appendix U and scholastic.com/NSFIntervention).
The day before the event	• Send a prerecorded phone message to every K–2 parent (Appendix V and scholastic.com/NSFIntervention). • Print the "Take me to RISE With Literacy tonight at _____ P.M." stickers. • Purchase refreshments, such as cookies and juice.

 The Next Step Forward in Reading Intervention © 2018 by Jan Richardson and Ellen Lewis. Published by Scholastic Inc.

Countdown to RISE With Literacy

When	What to Do
The day of the event _Before_ the end of the school day	• Send every child home wearing a "Take me to RISE With Literacy tonight at _____ P.M." sticker.
After the end of the school day and before the event	• Prepare the Stations: **Station 1:** Set up the projector, load the PowerPoint at scholastic.com/NSFIntervention, test the sound system, and arrange chairs. If needed, ensure a translator is present. **Station 2:** Make sure each classroom has a read-aloud book as well as copies of guided reading books and the Comprehension Card on tables. **Station 3:** Set up tables for refreshments and for take-home books. • Post signs directing parents to each station.
During the event	• Be visible and available. Greet parents, visit the classrooms, and troubleshoot issues.

The success of RISE With Literacy is based on the power of partnership. When we invite students, parents, siblings, teachers, and administrators to work together to understand what literacy is and how to achieve it, we open a world of possibilities—a world where schools and communities unite for a common purpose. We create a world where students become proficient, engaged readers who can't wait to read their next book. We enrich the lives of all children and their families with the joy of reading. RISE together!

CLOSING THOUGHTS

At the beginning of this book, we told you that RISE stands for "Reading Intervention for Students to Excel." But after completing the intervention himself—and making huge gains—one student, named Mason, decided to change what the acronym stands for to "Reading Is So Exciting."

Reading is exciting when children master the skills they need to become proficient and joyful readers. It literally changes their lives. RISE and RISE Up have made a profound difference for thousands of kids like Mason. We're confident you will see the same results with your students.

Go to scholastic.com/NSFIntervention to see the exciting findings of an ongoing action research study. We are actively collecting and analyzing data, and updating the study at the end of each grading period. We believe you'll be as excited by the results as we are!

Mason and his RISE sign

REFERENCES

Allington, R. (2009). *What really matters in fluency: Research-based practices across the curriculum*. Boston: Pearson.

Bear, D., Invernizzi, M., Templeton, S., & Johnston, F. (2015). *Words their way: Word study for phonics, vocabulary, and spelling instruction, 6th edition*. Boston: Pearson.

Beaver, J. (2012). *Developmental reading assessment, 2nd edition plus*. Boston: Pearson.

Fountas, I. & Pinnell, G. S. (2016). *Benchmark assessment system*. Portsmouth, NH: Heinemann.

Goswami, U., & Bryant, P. (1990). *Phonological skills and learning to read: Essays in developmental psychology*. Hillside, NJ: Earlbaum.

Harvey, S. & Ward, A. (2017). *From striving to thriving: How to grow confident, capable readers*. New York: Scholastic.

Richardson, J. (2016). *The next step forward in guided reading: An assess-decide-guide framework for supporting every reader*. New York: Scholastic.

Richardson, J., & Walther, M. P. (2013). *Next step guided reading assessment: Grades K–2*. New York: Scholastic.

Richardson, J., & Walther, M. P. (2013). *Next step guided reading assessment: Grades 3–6*. New York: Scholastic.

Zinke, S. (2017). *Rime magic: Phonics-powered prevention and intervention for all students*. New York: Scholastic.

APPENDICES

Appendices can be downloaded from scholastic.com/NSFIntervention.

RISE Station 1 Lesson Plan: Read a New Book

Students read a new book with teacher prompting.

Book Title	Level	Date

Brief Synopsis

New Vocabulary and Language

_____ _____ _____ _____

Monitoring and Word-Solving Prompts

☐ Are you right?

☐ Does that make sense (or look right)?

☐ Reread and sound the first part.

☐ What would make sense and look right?

☐ Check the middle (or end) of the word.

☐ Find the magic rime.

☐ Cover the ending. Find a part you know.

☐ Do you know another word that looks like this one?

☐ Try the other vowel sound.

☐ Use a known part.

☐ Look all the way to the end of the word.

See _The Next Step Forward in Guided Reading_, pages 125 and 178, for additional prompts.

Fluency Prompts

☐ Don't point. Read it faster.

☐ Read it the way the character would say it.

☐ Read that again while I use my fingers to frame a few words at a time.

☐ How would you say that bold word?

☐ Did you notice that period (or question mark)? Read that again.

☐ Read it while I use my finger to help you read a bit faster. (Use finger to mask the text.)

Comprehension Prompts

☐ What did you read?

☐ What are you thinking?

☐ What's the problem in the story?

☐ How is the character feeling now? Why?

☐ What have you learned?

RISE Station 1 Lesson Plan: Read a New Book

Take mini-records. Record observations and next steps for individual students.

Name:	Name:
Name:	Name:
Name:	Name:
Name:	Name:
Name:	Name:
Name:	Name:
Name:	Name:
Name:	Name:

Notes From Daily Debriefing

RISE Station 2 Lesson Plan: Phonics and Word Study

Review known sight words, teach a new word, and do word study activities to teach phonemic awareness and phonics skills.

Word Study Focus	Date

Learn Sight Words (4–5 minutes)

Review three familiar words (writing):

_____   _____   _____

Teach one new sight word: _____

Do steps 1–4 in order:

1. What's Missing?
2. Mix and Fix
3. Table Writing
4. Write and Retrieve

Rime Magic for RISE: Step _____ (3–5 minutes)

Word Study Options (5–7 minutes)

☐ Picture Sorting _____

☐ Making Words _____

☐ Sound Boxes _____

☐ Analogy Charts _____

☐ Breaking Words _____

☐ Make a Big Word _____

☐ Make Spelling/Meaning Connections _____

RISE Station 2 Lesson Plan: Phonics and Word Study

Record observations and next steps for individual students.

Name:	Name:
Name:	Name:
Name:	Name:
Name:	Name:
Name:	Name:
Name:	Name:
Name:	Name:
Name:	Name:

Notes From Daily Debriefing

RISE Station 3 Lesson Plan: Reread Yesterday's Book

Reread and discuss yesterday's book.

Book Title	Level	Date

Comprehension Focus

Monitoring and Word-Solving Prompts

☐ Are you right? Does it make sense? Does it look right?

☐ Reread and sound the first part.

☐ What would make sense and look right?

☐ Check the middle (or end) of the word.

☐ Cover the ending. Find a part you know.

☐ Do you know another word that looks like this one?

☐ Try the other vowel sound.

☐ Use a known part.

☐ Look all the way to the end of the word.

See *The Next Step Forward in Guided Reading*, pages 125 and 178, for additional prompts.

Fluency Prompts

☐ Don't point. Read it faster.

☐ Read it the way the character would say it.

☐ I'll frame the words. You read them together.

☐ Attend to punctuation.

Comprehension Discussion Starters

☐ Beginning-Middle-End (B-M-E)

☐ Connections

☐ Problem-Solution

☐ Story Retelling Rope

☐ Shared Retelling

☐ Somebody-Wanted-But-So (SWBS)

☐ Green Questions

☐ Red Questions

☐ Compare & Contrast

☐ Character Feelings and Traits

☐ Very Important Part (V.I.P.)

RISE Station 3 Lesson Plan: Reread Yesterday's Book

Record observations and next steps for individual students.

Name:	Name:
Name:	Name:
Name:	Name:
Name:	Name:
Name:	Name:
Name:	Name:
Name:	Name:
Name:	Name:

Notes From Daily Debriefing

RISE Station 4 Lesson Plan: Guided Writing

Write about yesterday's new book.

Book Title	Level	Date

Dictated Sentences or Writing Prompt

Guided Writing Response Options for Levels E–N

☐ Beginning-Middle-End (B-M-E)

☐ Problem-Solution

☐ New Facts You Learned

☐ Somebody-Wanted-But-So (SWBS)

☐ Track a Character's Feelings

☐ Describe a Character's Traits

☐ V.I.P. (Very Important Part of the Story)

☐ Compare & Contrast

☐ Five-Finger Retell

☐ Write Questions and Answer Them

☐ Other:

Plan for Writing

(List key words or create graphic organizer.)

Target Skills

(List skills to teach today.)

RISE Station 4 Lesson Plan: Guided Writing

Record observations and next steps for individual students.

Name:	Name:
Name:	Name:
Name:	Name:
Name:	Name:
Name:	Name:
Name:	Name:
Name:	Name:
Name:	Name:

Notes From Daily Debriefing

RISE Up Intervention Lesson Plan

Station 1: Read a New Text for Literal Comprehension

Text Title:	Date:	Comprehension Focus (Strategies 1–4 listed on page 85):

Synopsis of the Text:

New Vocabulary: (Steps: 1. Define 2. Connect 3. Relate to Book 4. Turn & Talk)

Read With Prompting
Using Module

_____

Station 2: Reread Yesterday's Text for Deeper Comprehension

Text Title:	Date:	Comprehension Focus (Strategies 5–12 listed on page 85):

Read With Prompting
Using Module

_____

Station 3: Reread Yesterday's Text for Deeper Comprehension or Do Guided Writing

Text Title:	Date:	Comprehension Focus (Strategies 5–12 listed on page 85):

Read With Prompting
Using Module

_____

Guided Writing Prompt:

RISE Up Intervention Lesson Plan

Observations: Record each student's understanding of the strategy, using this rubric:
(1) Not Independent   (2) Somewhat Independent   (3) Almost Independent   (4) Independent

Name:	Name:
Name:	Name:
Name:	Name:
Name:	Name:
Name:	Name:
Name:	Name:

Next Steps

RISE Up Classroom Lesson Plan

Text Title:	Dates:

Day 1: Read a New Text for Literal Comprehension

Comprehension Focus (Strategies 1–4 listed on page 85):	Module # _____

Synopsis of the Text:

New Vocabulary: (Steps: 1. Define 2. Connect 3. Relate to Book 4. Turn & Talk)

Read With Prompting. Discussion Prompt:

Day 1 or 2: Independent Writing

Writing Prompt:

Day 2: Reread the Text for Deeper Comprehension

Comprehension Focus (Strategies 5–12 listed on page 85):	Module # _____

Read With Prompting. Discussion Prompt:

RISE Up Classroom Lesson Plan

Observations: Record each student's understanding of the strategy, using this rubric:
(1) Not Independent   (2) Somewhat Independent   (3) Almost Independent   (4) Independent

Name:	Name:
Name:	Name:
Name:	Name:

Next Steps

Sight Word Charts for Monitoring Progress

Sight Word Chart for Monitoring Progress—Level C

	Student 1	Student 2	Student 3	Student 4
and				
are				
come				
for				
got				
here				
not				
play				
said				
you				

Sight Word Chart for Monitoring Progress—Level D

	Student 1	Student 2	Student 3	Student 4
day				
down				
into				
looking				
she				
they				
went				
where				
will				
your				

Sight Word Charts for Monitoring Progress

Sight Word Chart for Monitoring Progress—Level E

	Student 1	Student 2	Student 3	Student 4
all				
away				
back				
big				
her				
over				
this				
want				
who				
with				

Sight Word Chart for Monitoring Progress—Level F

	Student 1	Student 2	Student 3	Student 4
came				
have				
help				
next				
now				
one				
some				
then				
was				
what				

Sight Word Charts for Monitoring Progress

Sight Word Chart for Monitoring Progress—Levels G, H, and I

	Student 1	Student 2	Student 3	Student 4
Set 1				
didn't				
don't				
eat				
from				
give				
good				
make				
of				
out				
saw				
were				
when				
Set 2 (more challenging)				
again				
because				
could				
does				
every				
laugh				
many				
new				
night				
very				
walk				
why				

Word Knowledge Inventory

Student _____ Date _____

Directions: Dictate the following words as the student writes them on a blank sheet of paper. Then circle the skills that need further instruction.

Word Knowledge Inventory								
	Short Vowel	Digraph	Initial Blend	Final Blend	Long Vowel VCe	Vowel Team Diphthong	R-controlled vowel	Inflectional ending
1. grab	a		gr					
2. sled	e		sl					
3. chin	i	ch						
4. shot	o	sh						
5. thud	u	th						
6. brick			br	-ck				
7. plump			pl	-mp				
8. skunk			sk	-nk				
9. clasp			cl	-sp				
10. stroke			str		o-e			
11. twine			tw		i-e			
12. quake			qu		a-e			
13. stark			st				ar	
14. thorn			th				or	
15. squirt			squ				ir	
16. snare			sn		-are			
17. drain			dr			ai		
18. gleam			gl			ea		
19. croak			cr			oa		
20. fright			fr			igh		
21. blowing			bl			ow		ing
22. talked						alk		ed (/t/)
23. sprouted			spr			ou		ed (/ed/)
24. spoil			sp			oi		
25. prowled			pr			ow		ed (/d/)
26. flapped			fl					-pped doubling feature
27. tries			tr					y to i add -es
28. hiking								e drop
Activities	picture sorts, making words, and sound boxes				analogy charts			

Teach a New Sight Word (3 minutes)

From the text, select a new sight word that students don't know how to write.
Refer to the Sight Word Charts (Appendix G and scholastic.com/NSFIntervention)
to identify words to teach at each level.

Step 1: What's Missing?

Write the word on a dry-erase board.

- Ask students to look at each letter as you slide an index card left to right across the word.

- Turn the board toward you. Erase a letter. Show the board to the students. Ask, "What's missing?" When students say the missing letter, write it back into the word. Repeat, erasing more letters until the whole word is erased.

- Have students call out each of the word's letters in order as you write them on the board.

Step 2: Mix and Fix

Give students magnetic letters to make the new word.

- Keep the word on the dry-erase board in case students need a reference.

- After students make the word, have them slide their finger under the word to check it for accuracy while saying the word. (Discourage them from segmenting each sound.)

- Have them push the letters up one at a time.

- Have students mix up the letters and remake the word, from left to right.

- Keep the word on the table and cover it with an index card.

Step 3: Table Writing

Ask students to "write" the word on the table with their index finger.
Make sure they are looking at their finger while they write.

Step 4: Write and Retrieve

Have students write the new word on a dry-erase board as they say it softly.

- Do not allow students to spell or sound out the word. You want them to learn it as a complete unit. After they write the word, have them erase it.

- Dictate a very familiar word they know how to write. Check and erase.

- Dictate the new sight word for them to retrieve from memory and write.

Rime Magic for RISE

See pages 29 to 30 for details on how to carry out the activity.

Short Vowel Strip for Step 1

Rimes for Step 1: Reading Magic Rimes. Write each two-letter rime on a 3-x-5 card.

ab	at	id	ob	ub
ad	ed	ig	od	ud
ag	em	im	og	ug
am	en	in	op	um
an	et	ip	ot	un
ap	ib	it	om	ut

Rime Magic for RISE

One-Syllable Words for Steps 2 and 3: Spelling, Writing, and Reading Words With Magic Rimes

Dictate some of the following words for students to spell and write (Step 2).

Write some of the words on 3-x-5 cards for students to read (Step 3).

Rime	Words With Magic Rimes
ab	cab, dab, gab, lab, crab, flab, grab, drab
ad	dad, had, lad, pad, sad, brad, clad, chad
ag	bag, lag, wag, flag, snag, brag, drag, shag
am	ham, jam, ram, yam, clam, spam, tram
an	ban, fan, pan, ran, than, plan, span, bran
ap	cap, lap, nap, tap, trap, slap, strap, chap
at	bat, mat, vat, chat, that, flat, slat, spat
ed	bed, red, wed, led, fed, shed, sled, shred
em	hem, gem, stem, them
en	den, hen, men, pen, ten, glen, then
et	bet, set, let, wet, fret
ib	bib, fib, rib, crib
id	bid, did, kid, lid, rid, grid, slid, skid, squid
ig	big, dig, fig, pig, wig, zig, brig, swig, twig
im	dim, him, rim, vim, slim, swim, brim, trim

Rime	Words With Endings
in	bin, fin, win, tin, chin, grin, shin, twin, skin
ip	dip, hip, rip, yip, clip, drip, grip, trip, quip
it	bit, fit, lit, hit, wit, grit, quit, spit, twit
ob	cob, mob, sob, blob, glob, slob, snob
od	nod, pod, rod, sod, clod, plod, shod, trod
og	bog, dog, fog, jog, clog, frog, smog
om	mom, tom, prom
op	hop, top, chop, crop, drop, shop, slop, stop
ot	dot, got, rot, blot, clot, plot, shot, trot
ub	cub, rub, tub, grub, scrub, shrub, stub
ud	bud, cud, mud, thud, stud, spud
ug	bug, hug, rug, chug, drug, slug, shrug
um	hum, chum, drum, glum, slum, plum, strum
un	bun, fun, pun, run, shun, spun, stun
ut	but, cut, gut, hut, jut, nut, shut, strut

Rime Magic for RISE

Words for Steps 4 and 5: Spelling, Writing, and Reading Words With Endings

Write the following endings on an 8-x-2 card for students to read.

Endings Card

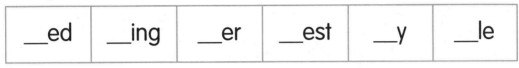

| __ed | __ing | __er | __est | __y | __le |

Dictate some of the following words for students to spell and write (Step 4).

Write some of the words on 8-x-2 cards for students to read (Step 5).

Rime	Words With Endings
ab	crabby, shabby, grabbed, scrabble
ad	padded, sadder, saddest, ladder
ag	bragging, stagger, dragging, wagged
am	crammed, slammed, hammer, slamming
an	planned, spanning, scanner, nanny
ap	trapping, strapped, clapped, snapper
at	chatted, flattest, splatter, scattered
ed	wedding, sledding, shredded, shredder
em	hemmed, stemming, hemming
en	penny, plenty, twenty
et	betting, setter, wettest, fretted
ib	fibbing, dribble, scribble
id	skidded, middle, kidding

Rime	Words With Endings
ig	bigger, biggest, giggle, squiggle
im	slimmest, swimmer, trimmed, shimmer
in	grinned, skinny, spinner, grinning
ip	chipped, slipper, tripping, stripping
it	quitter, spitting, twitter, splitting
ob	clobber, sobbed, robbing, snobby
od	oddest, plodded, shoddy, nodding
og	jogging, clogged, foggy, goggles
om	mommy
op	chopped, dropping, shopper, sloppy
ot	bottle, rotted, throttle, trotting
ub	clubbed, scrubbing, stubbed, rubber
ud	budding, muddy, shudder
ug	buggy, hugger, shrugged, struggle
um	summer, chummy, drummer, strumming
un	funny, running, runny, stunned
ut	putter, strutting, clutter, butter

Adapted from Zinke, S. *Rime Magic,* 2017. Scholastic.

Sound Box Template

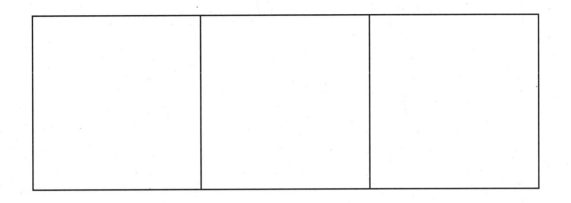

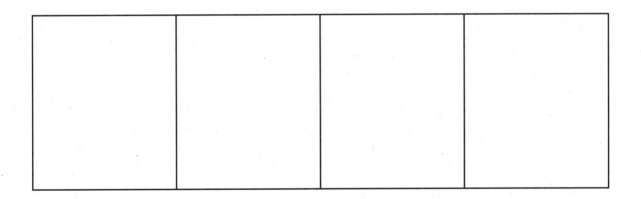

Analogy Chart Template

Examples for the Make Spelling/Meaning Connections Activity

Feature	Examples
-ful	wonderful, meaningful, mouthful
-ity	activity, quality, ability
-ment	argument, compartment, apartment
-ness	kindness, goodness, happiness
-ous	wondrous, generous, dangerous
-sion	mansion, confusion, comprehension
-tion	vacation, station, adoption
-ture	picture, adventure, capture
con-	conduct, contest, conclusion
dis-	dislike, distrust, discover
ex-	expand, explain, exhale
mis-	mistake, misbehave, misunderstand
non-	nonsense, nonviolent, nonfat
pre-	preview, predict, prehistoric
pro-	protect, protest, provide
re-	repeat, reread, review
sub-	submerge, subject, subtract
tele-	telephone, telescope, television
trans-	transfer, transform, transport
un-	unhappy, unhealthy, unhelpful
graph	graphic, photograph, autograph

Story Retelling Rope

Directions: Copy the figures onto a piece of card stock. Cut out the figures and staple them in order down the length of a 15- to 24-inch piece of ribbon.

#1 Title

#2 Setting/Where?

#3 Characters/Who?

#4 Problem/What is the problem in the story?

#5 Three Most Important Events

#6 Solution/Outcome

Shared Retelling Cards

In the beginning . . .	Next . . .
The problem is . . .	After that . . .
Then . . .	Finally . . .

Guided Writing Page Template (Levels C–E)

a b c d e f g h i j k l m n o p q r s t u v w x y z

Guided Writing Page Template (Levels F–I)

a b c d e f g h i j k l m n o p q r s t u v w x y z

Guided Writing Page Template (Levels J–N)

n o p q r s t u v w x y z

a b c d e f g h i j k l m

Character Feelings and Traits Charts (Levels C–I)

Feeling: How does the character feel now? **Trait:** How does the character act most of the time?

Happy	Sad	Mad	Good
glad	unhappy	angry	kind
joyful	sorry	upset	helpful
proud	hurt	cross	safe
merry	gloomy	grumpy	friendly
thrilled	lonely	grouchy	thankful
pleasant	hopeless	moody	caring
excited	ashamed	cranky	polite

Scared	Mean	Brave	Other
afraid	selfish	unafraid	lazy
frightened	rude	bold	clever
nervous	cruel	fearless	hopeful
shy	greedy	daring	bored
worried	nasty	confident	curious

Character Feelings and Traits Charts (Levels J–N)

Feeling: How does the character feel now? **Trait:** How does the character act most of the time?

Happy	Sad	Mad	Good
overjoyed	disappointed	furious	respectful
delighted	discouraged	irritated	thoughtful
terrific	depressed	displeased	patient
cheerful	sorrowful	touchy	generous
optimistic	miserable	annoyed	gracious
elated	melancholy	aggravated	faithful

Scared	Mean	Brave	Other
terrified	hateful	courageous	responsible
anxious	unfair	determined	impatient
confused	ungrateful	adventurous	embarrassed
panicked	dishonest	plucky	concerned

Comprehension Cards

MODULE 1

Fix-Up Strategies

When you are confused . . .

- reread or read on.
- ask yourself a question.
- use text features.
- make a connection.
- replace words you don't know with words that make sense.

MODULE 2

STP

Stop—Stop reading; cover the text.

Think—What did I read?

Paraphrase—Put in your own words.

MODULE 3

B-M-E

What happened at the beginning, middle, and end?

At the beginning _____.

In the middle _____.

At the end _____.

MODULE 4

Five-Finger Retell

MODULE 5

Key Words

- As you read, write one or two important words.
- Use those words to summarize the text.

MODULE 6

Who-What

Who is the most important character?

What did he or she do?

MODULE 7

Vocabulary Strategies

1. Reread (or read on) and look for clues.
2. Use the picture to explain the word.
3. Use a known part.
4. Make a connection.
5. Substitute a word that makes sense.
6. Use the glossary.

MODULE 8

Green Questions

I must go to the text and find the answer.

Who . . . ?   When . . . ?

What . . . ?   How . . . ?

Where . . . ?   Which . . . ?

MODULE 9

Red Questions

I must stop and think about the answer.

Why . . . ?

Why do you think . . . ?

How . . . ?

What if . . . ?

MODULE 10

V.I.P.
Fiction

Action—What is the most important thing the character did?

Feeling—What is the most important feeling the character had?

MODULE 11

V.I.P.
Nonfiction

1. Flag an important fact or sentence.
2. Write a few key words.
3. Use the key words to write a main idea statement.

MODULE 12

Main Idea/Details

1. Turn the heading into a question.
2. Bullet key words that answer the question.
3. Use the question and key words to identify the main idea of the passage.

Comprehension Cards

MODULE 13

Track the Character's Feelings

How did the character feel at the beginning, middle, and end?

The character felt _____ because _____.

MODULE 14

Character–Trait–Evidence

What trait describes the character? What is your evidence?

Character	Trait	Evidence

The character is _____. In the story she (or he) _____.

MODULES 14 AND 26

Form an Opinion— SOAR

S—State opinion

O—Offer reasons

A—Add examples

R—Restate opinion

MODULE 15

Who-What-Why

Who is the most important character?

What did he or she do?

Why did he or she do that?

MODULE 16

Action-Motivation

- Find an important action a character takes.
- Write why the character takes it (motivation).

MODULE 17

Create a Sociogram

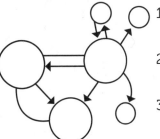

1. Identify characters.
2. Draw circles and lines.
3. Describe relationships.

Comprehension Cards

MODULE 18

Yellow Questions

I must slow down and look for the answer.

How are _____ and _____ similar?

How are _____ and _____ different?

What caused . . . ?

What was the effect of . . . ?

MODULES 18, 19, AND 28

Compare & Contrast

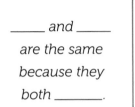

____ and ____ are the same because they both _____.	____ and ____ are different because one is ____ but the other is _____.

MODULE 19

Cause-Effect

1. Find an important event.
2. Write a "what caused" or "why" question.

   What caused _____?

   Why _____?
3. Answer your question.

MODULE 20

Inferences From Dialogue

- Find an important or surprising dialogue.
- What was the character thinking?
- What are you thinking?
- Write your inference.

MODULE 21

Inferences From Actions

- Find an important or surprising action.
- What was the character thinking?
- What are you thinking?
- Write your inference.

MODULE 22

Inferences From Inner Thoughts

- Find a sentence where the author tells what the character is thinking.
- What are you thinking?
- Write your inference.

Comprehension Cards

MODULES 20, 21, AND 22

Make an Inference: Fiction

1. Find an important or surprising dialogue or action.
2. Why did the character say or do that?
3. What is the character thinking?
4. What are you thinking?

I'm thinking _____ *because the character* _____.

MODULE 23

Draw Conclusions

Use clues from the text and what you know to make an inference.

I read . . . . I know . . . . I conclude . . . .

If . . . then . . . .

MODULE 24

SWBS

_____ wanted _____
   (somebody)

but _____ so _____.

Then _____.

MODULE 25

Key Word Summary

What were the most important words?

_____

_____

_____

_____

Use the key words to write a summary.

MODULE 26

Thesis-Proof

Thesis Statement	
Support	Oppose
Summary	

MODULE 27

Text Features

- Flag a text feature.
- Why did the author include this text feature?
- Write a question that can be answered from the text feature.
- Repeat with other text features.
- Share your questions with the group.

Comprehension Cards

MODULE 28

Text Structure

- Read the passage and identify the text structure.
- Draw the graphic organizer below that matches that structure, and record your notes.

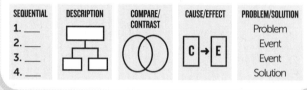

MODULE 28

Problem-Solution

Record key words.

Problem	Solution

The problem was _____.

The problem was solved _____.

MODULE 29

Reciprocal Teaching

Predict: What will you read next?
I predict I will learn . . . because . . . .

Clarify: What confused you?
At first, I didn't understand . . . so I . . . .

Question: What were you wondering?
I wonder . . . . How . . . ? What would happen if . . . ?

Summarize: Summarize what you read.
This passage is about . . . .

MODULES 8, 9, 18, AND 19

Ask Green, Red, and Yellow Questions

As you read, ask different kinds of questions.

Green	Red	Yellow
Who...?	I wonder...?	What caused...?
What...?	Why...?	What was the effect of...?
When...?	What would happen if...?	How are ____ and ____ similar or different?
Where...?		
Which...?		

STRATEGY 10

Evaluating Nonfiction

- What is the author's purpose?
- What is the central idea?
- Why did the author write this text?
- Why did the author include this [text feature]?
- What are the facts and opinions?
- Do you agree (or disagree) with the author? Why?

STRATEGY 10

Evaluating Fiction

- What is the theme or moral?
- How did the character change?
- What did the character learn?
- What lesson did you learn?
- What message is hidden in this story?
- What character, animal, place, or object symbolizes an important idea? Draw it.

My Word Wall

A
about animals
afraid another
after answer
again around
although asked
always

B
beautiful between
because bought
been buy
before
beginning
believe

C
called could
care course
carried cried
caught
children
coming

D
decided dropped
didn't during
different
does
doesn't
don't

E
enough
especially
every
except
excited
exciting

F
favorite
finally
first
found
friend
frightened

G
getting guess
girl
give
goes
gone
good

H
happy
happened
hear
heard
how
however

I
if
I'll
interesting
it's (it is)

J
jumped
just

K
kept
knew
know
known

L
laughed loose
learned lose
little
looked

M
many
middle
might
more
mother

N
named none
need now
new
night

O
of other
off our
often
once
one only

P
people
perfect
piece
place
pretty
probably

Q
quick
quiet
quite

R
ready
really
receive
right
running

S
said sure
saw surprised
scared
since
special
stopped

T
terrible thought
their threw
there touch
they tried
they're trouble
(they are)
though

U
until
upon
use
usual
usually

V
very

W
walk went
wanted were
was with
water would
wear write

Wh
what who
when why
where
which
while

Y
year
young
your
you're (you are)

Word-Solving Strategies Card

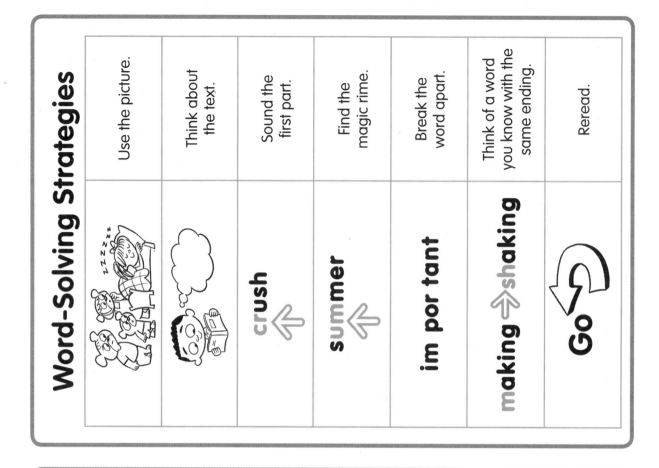

Word-Solving Strategies

Use the picture.	
Think about the text.	
Sound the first part.	crush ⇐
Find the magic rime.	summer ⇐
Break the word apart.	im por tant
Think of a word you know with the same ending.	making ⇒ shaking
Reread.	Go

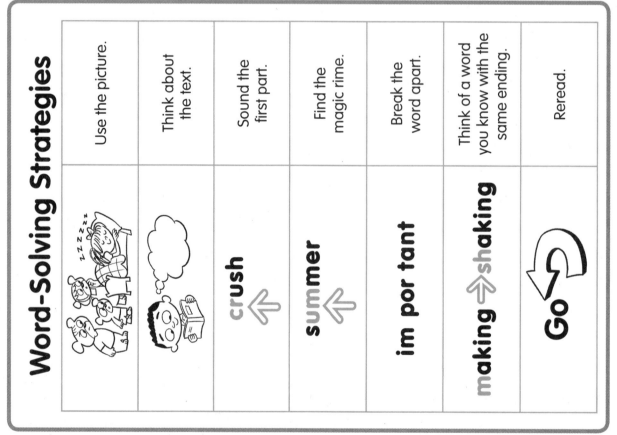

Word-Solving Strategies

Use the picture.	
Think about the text.	
Sound the first part.	crush ⇐
Find the magic rime.	summer ⇐
Break the word apart.	im por tant
Think of a word you know with the same ending.	making ⇒ shaking
Reread.	Go

RISE With Literacy: Letter to Parents

Dear Parent,

Please take me to the "RISE With Literacy" night at school. We'll learn something to help me be a better reader, and I'm going to get a free book. Other family members can come, too. The "RISE With Literacy" night is coming soon. Let's put it in our calendar!

Date: _____ Time: _____

Where: _____

✂ -

RSVP

We're coming to the "RISE With Literacy" night to work on reading skills with our child.

Name of student: _____ Grade: _____

Number of family members attending the event: _____

_____
Signature

RISE With Literacy: Phone Message Script

RISE With Literacy

Hello, this is _____ from _____ (name of school).

I am calling on behalf of the teachers and administrators to invite you to attend the "RISE With Literacy" night tomorrow evening _____ (day of week), _____ (date), from _____ (start and end times, one hour).

RISE With Literacy is our family literacy program for parents, students, and siblings. We will show you some wonderful strategies to help your children increase their literacy skills at home. You will work together practicing some of those strategies.

We look forward to seeing you and your children tomorrow evening. Every student will receive a free book, and there will be refreshments for all!

It's TOMORROW night at _____ (start time). See you then!

Thank you.

Have a translator repeat the script in Spanish, if necessary.

INDEX

Rime Magic

by Sharon Zinke

Phonics-Powered **Prevention** and **Intervention** for **All Students**

In engaging five-minute lessons, students combine onsets and endings with rimes to create words—like magic!—and then analyze their patterns. These rime lessons help students "crack the code" of the written word, and when practiced repeatedly, bolster reading and spelling proficiency.

> *It's phenomenal how much progress our students have made in **such a short time**. It's amazing!*
> —Kim Watts, Principal

Phonics-Powered **Prevention** and **Intervention** for All Students

SHARON ZINKE

Rime Magic

SHARON ZINKE

Rime Magic TEACHER'S GUIDE

Rime Magic POWER PAK

Frog and Toad Are Friends

Story and pictures by ARNOLD LOBEL

3 Trade Books **& more!**

ank
ip

80 Magic Rime Cards

thankful
slipper

175 Embedded Rime Cards

The Next Step Forward in Reading Intervention © 2018 by Jan Richardson and Ellen Lewis. Published by Scholastic Inc.